I0516886

Fallacies

Part 3, Book 4 of
Summa Logicae

William of Ockham

Foreword by Peter King,
Professor of Philosophy and of Mediaeval
Studies, Department of Philosophy,
University of Toronto, CA.

Translated by Richard Robinson

Sunny Lou Publishing Company
Portland, Oregon, USA
http://www.sunnyloupublishing.com

Revised: 2025 August 11
Original Publication Date: 2025 May 31

ISBN: 978-1-955392-76-1

This translation from Latin is based on
De Fallaciis, Pars III, Tractatus Quartus of *Summa Logicae*, in *Opera Philosophica I of Guillelmi de Ockham, Opera Philosophica et Theologica*, Editiones Instituti Franciscani Universitatis S. Bonaventurae, St. Bonaventure, N.Y., 1974.

Contents

Translator's Preface

I am not a logician, although I like to think of myself as logical. In the profession I used to profess, logic was central to success. Nor am I a medievalist, although I sometimes fancy myself one. Assuredly, I am a better medievalist today than I was (or pretended to be) six months ago.

This translation of William of Ockham's *Fallacies,* – or rather, Part 3, Book 4 of the *Summa Logicae*, Ockham's important treatise on syllogistic logic – was born of an interest in nominalism. That interest in nominalism was sparked by the translation last year of *Antisthenes: The Founder of Cynicism.* Antisthenes, as it turns out, at least according to Charles Chappuis, was the protonominalist, due in large part to his philosophical disagreements with fellow student Plato and this latter's theory of ideas, or universals, having an extra-mental existence.

All fascinating and mysterious stuff. All the more fascinating when, after doing research on nominalism – what it actually means, what it is about, and how it came to be in the first place, not to mention what problems it aspires to solve – I came across a medieval predecessor of William of Ockham's, Peter Abelard, a brilliant philosopher (so I'm told), theologian, logician, and nominalist (or conceptualist) in his own right. Suffice it to say that there is reason to believe, or at least there is the scrap of a thread of a theory, which I am still pulling on, that nominalism developed initially as a means to solve, logically, using syllogistic, the problem of the Trinity.

Now, that is super interesting! And one need's that fascination and interest – as well as many cups of strong coffee, and patience, and good health – in order to work one's way through the sometimes dense, dry, and often arcane material. Which is often true, the dryness is, of any subject matter worth the effort to learn and keep the candles burning at night.

On a lesser scale, this translation was also born of a long-standing interest in fallacy, and the nature of fallacy, which I blame squarely on a perduring interest in Socrates, the man and the myth, and his (or Plato's) dialectic. Admitting too that when in the past Plato was read, I would take his (or Socrates') word for it that their logical arguments made sense. My blind trust in their sharper instruments could be chalked up to naïvety, youthful intellectual laziness, and also a lack of knowledge and training in formal logic. So much for confessions.

With that out of the way, and unless you are a scholar of medieval philosophy and logic, the reader of this *Fallacies* may find, as I found, that a certain amount of preparatory (or simultaneous) reading material will be immensely helpful in understanding many of the terms and concepts about terms and concepts on which this work is based. Which includes most of the material in the *Summa Logicae* that precedes the *Fallacies*. I would recommend then, at the very least, the following works:

- Loux, Michael J. *Ockham's Theory of Terms, Part I of the* Summa Logicae. University of

Notre Dame Press, 1974.

- Freddoso, Alfred J. & Shuurman, Henry. *Ockham's Theory of Propositions: Part II of the Summa Logicae*. University of Notre Dame Press, 1980.

- Aristotle. *Organon.*

- King, Peter. "William of Ockham: Summa Logicae." In *Central Works of Philosophy* (Vol. 1). Acumen 2005:243–XXX.

- Spade, Paul Vincent. *Thoughts, Words and Things: An Introduction to Late Mediaeval Logic and Semantic Theory.* Version 1.2: December 27, 2007.

- Kneale, William, & Kneale, Martha. *The Development of Logic.* Oxford at the Clarendon Press, 1962.

– Richard Robinson, May 30, Joan of Arc's Feast Day.[1]

---

[1] All that preface without once mentioning "Occam's Razor"!

Foreword

By Peter King, Professor of Philosophy and of Mediaeval Studies, Department of Philosophy, University of Toronto, Canada.

Ockham's view of logic is more inclusive than ours. For Ockham, logic includes not only the study of formally valid inference – the sole concern of contemporary logic – but also the study and use of materially valid inferences, which hold in virtue of the meaning of their terms; topical inferences, which rely on general connections, such as reasoning from whole to part; and the study of fallacies, that is, the systematic analysis of what can go wrong in an argument. The proviso 'and use' is not idle: logic is not restricted to the mere study of abstract structures but also [includes] how the broader knowledge of correct kinds of reasoning is used in practice, on the one hand, to construct arguments and, on the other hand, to analyse them. A key part of analysis is diagnosis. The logician needs to know about fallacies in much the same way a doctor has to know about disease. Understanding healthy bodies or sound argumentation should be complemented as far as possible by understanding how they may go wrong: the germ theory of disease, for example, provides a systematic theory about the causes of certain kinds of illness; the theory of fallacies provides a systematic theory about the ways in which arguments fail to establish their (purported) conclusions. As Ockham puts it in his Introduction,[2] "the usefulness of this knowledge [of fallacies] is clear; for it is by this knowledge that invalid reasoning is detected in an argument erring in form, whereas without this knowledge it is impossible to detect."

Suppose, along with Ockham, that knowing about fallacies, or, better, knowing how to detect fallacies, is useful. What kind of knowledge is involved here? Ockham holds that it [is] knowledge that pertains to argumentation and that it is systematic. To say that fallacies pertain to argumentation is no small claim. Nowadays fallacies are taught in classes on 'informal logic' or critical reasoning, and often deal with rhetorical argumentative strategies, such as "poisoning the well" (casting aspersions on the source of the argument) or arguing *ad hominem* (against the person rather than the position); they also cover cognitive bias, hasty generalisation, appeals to authority, false dilemmas, and any number of bits of reasoning that someone holds to be unfounded: the Monte Carlo fallacy (treating independent events as connected), the naturalistic fallacy (defining the moral good through non-moral features), the pathetic fallacy (attributing human thoughts and feelings to non-human subjects). Whatever the pitfalls of such modes of reasoning, though, they are not Ockham's concern. Instead, Ockham takes a fallacy to be an error in an argument which prevents it from establishing its conclusion. Ockham, therefore, has what is sometimes called nowadays a 'formal' conception of fallacies, since they are flaws in what would otherwise be acceptable lines of reasoning – regardless of the dialectical

---

[2]Introduction: See Chapter 1, "On the Types of Fallacy," below.

(pragmatic) context in which they may occur, or their actual success in causing people to adopt their purported conclusions.

Ockham's account of fallacies, as noted, is systematic; it is a theory that attempts to classify all (formal) fallacies. It is not, in its outlines, a new theory. Ockham adopts the standard list of thirteen (formal) fallacies from Aristotle's logical works. Yet there are two ways in which Ockham pours this old wine into new bottles. Aristotle divides fallacies into those that are due to language ("in diction") and those that are due to extralinguistic features ("outside of diction"). Ockham rejects this venerable division. Rather, he says, the important distinction is between defects of reasoning that are due to the conventionalities of ordinary spoken or written languages, and those that are present even in thinking. This takes a bit of explanation. According to Ockham, the structure of thought is essentially linguistic; he goes so far as to refer to it as Mental Language, whose constituent elements (concepts) signify naturally. The concept of a weasel, for instance, naturally signifies a weasel; it does so in part from having been acquired through experience with actual weasels. These are the fundamental 'words' of Mental Language. Such words can, as in ordinary language, be combined with other words, and even joined together to make 'sentences' (thinking that something is so or that something is not so), which in turn can be strung together in reasoning – all in the mind, through mental operations of combination, division, judgment, and so on, powers which human beings possess by nature. Conventional languages such as English or Portuguese or Mandarin derive their meaning ultimately from Mental language; they are ways of encoding thoughts in written or spoken form. Ockham's correction of Aristotle, then, amounts to the claim that arguments can be defective due to their conventional expression, or they can more seriously be defective as the result of errors in thought itself.

Take for example the fallacy of equivocation: "Socrates is a human being; human being is a species; therefore, Socrates is a species" is fallacious because 'human being' is equivocal between a living rational animal in the first instance and an abstract classification in the second. The error arises because we use exactly the same expression in English in two rather different ways, or more exactly to stand for two different sorts of things. Our linguistic conventions have led us astray.

Could the same fallacy be present in Mental Language? According to Ockham, we think in Mental Language, so for this fallacy of equivocation to occur in Mental Language we would have to be having the thought of a human being as at once a living animal and as an abstract classification, which seems impossible: we may not always think clearly but we (usually? always?) know what we are thinking. In point of fact it is precisely questions such as this which bring us to the second way in which Ockham is philosophically an original departure from his Aristotelian sources. For Ockham sees that in such cases of equivocation the question is not simply what the word means, but how it can stand for what it signifies in the context of a sentence. Put another way, if signification maps roughly onto our contemporary notion of *meaning*, then spelling out what a term in a sentential context picks out maps roughly onto our contemporary notion of *reference*, a semantic property Ockham calls 'supposition' (which has nothing to do with 'supposing' something to be so). Ockham would say that the expression 'human being' in "Socrates is a human being" stands for the person Socrates, who is a human being; this is called 'personal supposition'. In "Human being is a species," by contrast, the same expression is used to stand not for some human person but instead for the abstract general thought of human being, that is, for the concept of human being; this is called 'simple supposition'. We also use words to stand for their inscription or utterance, as when we say "Human being is two words"; for obvious reasons, this is called 'material supposition'. Far and away the most common use is personal supposition, and Ockham devotes much effort earlier in the *Summa Logicae* to explaining how words stand for things in the sentential contexts (for example: the presence of the word 'all' makes a common term stand collectively for all the things for which [it] personally supposits). Ockham's explanation of fallacies is therefore more precise and capable of a much wider range than Aristotle's, and the theory of fallacies is the richer for it.

Ockham's philosophy has a contemporary freshness about it: he adopts something like the language-of-thought hypothesis; his philosophy of language allows for both semantic relations of meaning and reference, and thereby to truth; his view of logic itself includes modern logic as one of its subordinate parts, with an open-minded approach to reasoning, though one that insists on reasoning strictly speaking. Reading Ockham on fallacies, then, shows how practical logic can be – part of every philosopher's toolkit, since as he cautions us "it is impossible to have a perfect understanding of natural, moral, or any other science, without this knowledge [of fallacies]."

Fallacies

Chapter 1: On the Types of Fallacy

Now that we have spoken about arguments and types of argument [in the previous book], something about errors of argument and their consequences remains to be said. But these sorts of error are called fallacies, by which false arguments are in error. And so, we must now speak about fallacies; concerning which, first of all, some general comments are in order, to be followed by some particular cases.

First, then, it should be known that there are thirteen fallacies put forward by the Philosopher[3] and others, since every apparent and sophistical argument that errs in form does so by equivocation, or amphibology, or composition and division, or accent, or figure of speech, or accident, or *secundum quid et simpliciter*, or [affirming the] consequent, or irrelevant conclusion, as will be shown later when each fallacy is treated in particular, not to mention three others, in addition to those just mentioned, by which an opponent may err when arguing with a respondent. And because the Philosopher teaches how to avoid and detect an opponent's errors in argument, he enumerates thirteen fallacies.

Second, it should be known that some of these fallacies occur in diction, whereas others occur outside of diction. Six fallacies, then, occur in diction and seven outside of it. And it is to be noted that "diction" here

---

[3]The Philosopher: Aristotle.

refers not only to spoken words, but to any sign established by convention, whether spoken, written, or otherwise. And they are called fallacies in diction when an argument errs because of some conventional sign; so that anyone who makes a precise argument entirely in his mind, without using an idiomatic expression or commonly-accepted sign, would not be deceived by these fallacies. But such arguments cannot be made about all modes of such fallacy, although they can be made about a specific mode in some cases.

Other fallacies, however, which can be found in arguments composed of propositions existing only in the mind, – even if they contain no conventional sign, and however much the spoken or written arguments might exhibit consimilar defects – are called fallacies outside of diction.

And therefore it is false what some [people] say, that fallacies in diction result from speech and [that] fallacies outside of diction result from a thing or from the nature of a thing, because these are no more from the nature of a thing than those are. Rather, it must be said that fallacies in diction are those in which all arguments and only those arguments composed of conventional signs are in error, in all modes [of fallacy]; whereas fallacies outside of diction are those in which arguments composed of conventional signs, as well as those composed only of signs with naturally arising meanings, are in error.

Third, it should be noted that the logician, and not the sophist, needs to be familiar with these fallacies; indeed, he has to know the various general rules that are applicable to all bodies of knowledge, by which, together with the knowledge drawn from other domains, he can detect every false argument erring in form, regardless of the subject matter.

Wherefore, the usefulness of this knowledge is clear; for it is by this knowledge that invalid reasoning is detected in an argument erring in form, whereas without this knowledge it is impossible to detect. For which reason, it is impossible to have a perfect understanding of natural, moral, or any other science, without this knowledge. And therefore, those who are ignorant of this art and who intend to study other sciences, whether natural or moral philosophy, or even civil or canon law, or theology or any other discipline, if they should wish to teach or write extensively from what they have in their own head, beyond what is expressly found in sacred Scripture and in the writings of learned logicians, they will necessarily fall into many errors.

Hence, I do not doubt but that the multitude and contrariety of opinions, in theology as well as modern philosophy, may be attributed to the many, ignorant of logic, who have publicly taught new opinions, – beyond those things expressed in sacred Scripture and in the sayings of Saints and of Aristotle – and have left them behind in not a few notebooks.

Fourth, it should be known that, with respect to these fallacies, not only do paralogisms, strictly so-called – namely, those formed from two propositions and a conclusion, – err, but all false consequences do as well, whether they be enthymemes or inductions or examples, which may therefore be called paralogisms insofar as they can be reduced to a syllogism.

Chapter 2: On Equivocation and Its First Mode

Those observations having been made, it is now time to treat of specific fallacies. And to begin with, equivocation.

The first thing to say about equivocation is *what it is*; second, what its mode and form are with respect to the paralogism of equivocation; and third, how many modes of equivocation there are.

As for the first [point], it is said that equivocation is the diverse signification of some term used in a discourse, so that, according to some [people], the reason for the non-existence [of an argument's validity] is a diversity of signification. But this is not well said, for it is not always the case that where there is equivocation there is a diversity of signification. In fact, there can be equivocation in a purely univocal [term]; for example, the proposition "'man' is a noun" must be disambiguated on account of equivocation, even if the noun "man" meant only one thing, neither properly [i.e., literally] nor improperly [i.e., figuratively], and yet there is no diversity of signification here.

And, therefore, it must be said that equivocation is more aptly defined like this: it is a reference to many things under the same word or same sign. Where "reference" should not be taken here to mean signification but rather supposition or a standing-in for something else. And it should be understood what "a reference to many things" means in the aforesaid mode, or what it is denoted to mean, or not mean, because it is not always the case that, when there is equivocation, there is a term referring to different things; rather, sometimes the term is denoted to stand for diverse things and sometimes it is not. For example, if I were to say that "man is a species," it must be qualified because the term "man" can stand for many things, *scil*., for the intention of a soul, and for something external to a man. But if I were to say that "a white man was a man," – supposing that no man were ever white, the subject [of the sentence] does not stand for many things, *scil*., for those who were white or for these who are white, because no such person ever existed; instead, it is denoted to stand for such things in the negative [sense] of "there was no white man." For it is denoted to stand for such things under disjunction at least.

It must be understood, however, that "standing for diverse things" is not equivocation, but "standing for diverse things, so that [standing] for one thing and not [standing] for another" is equivocation. For example, in this [proposition,] "every man is an animal," "man" stands for diverse things, but it is not equivocation; but in the following proposition, "man is a species," "man" can stand for diverse things because it can stand for an intention [of the soul] and not for something external to it, or it can stand for something external to it and not for an intention; that is, someone might use this word for one thing and not for another.

From this it is clear that the cause of this apparent fallacy is the identity of a word or sign, the cause of non-existence [i.e., the argument's invalidity] is the diversity of usage, namely because it has to do with using it in one way or another.

As for the second [point], it should be known that the [proper] form of responding to such a paralogism should be this: that given a proposition with a single term capable of being interpreted in a variety of ways, that proposition must be disambiguated because such a term could be used in one way or in another. And so the response must either concede the argument or deny it, or concede it in one sense and deny it in another, or both concede it and deny it.

As for the third [point], it should be known that three modes of equivocation are posited. The first mode is when a term is equivocal by accident. It is said to be "equivocal by accident" when the term is made to signify equally and primarily – indeed, not always equally and primarily in time, but in intention – by many impositions, or by one [imposition] equivalent to many, so that one imposition is made to signify even though it [the term] had not been imposed previously. Just as happens when the same term is the same in different languages, like the word "me" in both Latin and English; it is therefore equivocal by accident. Thus is it frequently also [the case] with the same terms in the same language.

And it should be known that not only a term that signifies something in particular, like a categorematic term, but also a term that signifies nothing *per se* or in particular, but only consignifies, as syncategorematic terms do, can be equivocal, as will be shown in the case of adverbs, conjunctions, and other signs [of speech].

Secondly, it should be noted that any proposition in which such an equivocal term is posited should always be disambiguated by virtue of speaking, because otherwise it can be understood to be this or that, and either it is in one sense true and in another sense false, or it is in both senses false or in both senses true. But sometimes disputants can restrict the terms they use to a certain sense or a certain signification, and then disambiguation is not needed. This can be done by either convention or a certain arrangement between them. This can also be done through the addition of something; as if an opponent were to say: "I want that, whenever I add *a* to the word 'dog,' it should stand precisely for a barking animal." Then, if my opponent were to propose this proposition: "every dog *a* is a barking animal," disambiguation would not be needed; if, however, he should propose that "every dog is a barking animal," it would be needed. It can also be expressed without such additions; for example, if the opponent were to say this: "I want, throughout this debate, to take the noun 'dog' precisely for a barking animal." Then, whenever in this debate a proposition is put forward which includes the word "dog," disambiguation would not be needed.

And if someone asks whether such a proposition should be qualified [as] true or false, it must be said that by calling everything that is a subordinate sign of a true proposition in the mind "true," such a proposition should be qualified; if it has one sense that is true and another that is false, it is as much true as it is false, because it corresponds as much to a true proposition in the mind as to a false one. But [just] by calling something "true," to which a proposition in the mind precisely corresponds [as] true and not false – by accepting the designation in this way – does not make the proposition true or false.

And, therefore, when I said that the same proposition was true and false, necessary and impossible, and when [later] I said that it was not true and false, I accepted "true" and "false" equivocally in one place and in another. I understood it as equivocation then, although I did not express it, just as some writers do not always express the equivocations they give rise to in what they say.

According to the first mode [of equivocation], arguments like the following are in error – "every dog is an animal; a heavenly constellation is a dog; therefore a heavenly constellation is an animal" – for the major and minor [premises] should be distinguished, since "dog" in both can stand for a barking animal, and in that case the syllogism is valid, but the minor [premise] is false, namely, "a heavenly constellation is a dog." Or it [a dog] can stand as much in the major as in the minor for a heavenly constellation, and in that case the syllogism is valid, but the major premise is false, namely, "every dog is an animal," because then it is denoted that a heavenly constellation is an animal. Or "dog" can stand for a barking animal in the major premise and for a heavenly constellation in the minor, and in that case the syllogism is not valid but rather a fallacy of equivocation, because "dog" is understood equivocally in the major and minor premises.

Similarly, such a logical consequence [as the following] errs according to the fallacy of equivocation: "every dog is an animal, therefore a heavenly constellation is an animal" for the antecedent "every dog is an animal" must be distinguished, since "dog" can stand for a barking animal; and in that case the logical consequence is not valid, because then the argument proceeds from a term standing for one signification to the same term standing for another signification than this or that in the antecedent, as is manifestly apparent. If, however, "dog" should stand for a heavenly constellation in the antecedent, then the consequent is valid, because the argument proceeds from the term standing for one signification to that same signification, or, more properly speaking, to the same term standing for the same signification; and thus the logical consequence then is valid, but the antecedent is false. And this mode of responding, or something consimilar to it, ought to serve when responding to any argument in which a proposition is posited that must be distinguished with respect to any fallacy.

With respect to this mode [of equivocation], paralogisms such as the following are in error: "only water is in the vase; color is in the vase; therefore, color is water," for "in" can be understood in various and equivocal ways: in one way, it may denote something being in some place, just as [something] placed somewhere is said to be in a place, and so the major [premise] is true; in another way, in the minor [premise], it is understood to denote something being in some place like an accident in the subject. And just as equivocation occurs on account of the word "in," so too does equivocation frequently occur on account of other syncategorematic terms. When this happens, however, it is known through use and practice in the different sciences.

Chapter 3: On the Second Mode of Equivocation

Regarding the second mode of equivocation, it should be known that it occurs when the same term is principally and primarily made to signify or consignify some thing or things, and secondarily, on account of some attribution of another thing to the first significate, it is made to signify some other thing or things, such that we use the term in some propositions differently from how it was originally intended, though not in all [cases]. Just as with the noun "man," which was used primarily to signify rational animals, and, secondarily, on account of an image's likeness to a man, we use the noun "man" for an image in certain propositions; for example, in "a man is depicted," or in "a man is gold or silver" when the image is made out of gold or silver. In many other propositions, however, we do not use that word for its secondary signification; for example, in such propositions as "man runs," "man is an animal" and the like, we use the noun "man" for its primary signification and not for its secondary one.

From this arises a rule, which is that a proposition never needs to be disambiguated according to the second mode of equivocation unless that word, which can be understood equivocally in this way, is compared to something verifiably of secondary signification, or for some consimilar [reason]. And, therefore, [the proposition] "a man is depicted" needs to be disambiguated, but not "man runs," nor "man is an animal" and so forth. And the reason for this is that the term, wherever it is used, can stand for its primary significate, but it cannot always stand for its secondary significate, except in propositions where it compares to something verifiably of secondary signification. And for this reason such a proposition needs to be distinguished only according to the second mode of equivocation.

And if the cause and reason for this were looked into, it must be said that the principle reason for it is the will of users, and therefore if it pleased users, both [significations] could be distinguished, but this is not the [common] usage.

According to this mode, discourses such as the following err: "whatever runs, has feet; water runs; therefore, water has feet"; "every man is a rational animal; this image is a man; therefore, this image is a rational animal"; "the rock was Christ; therefore, something irrational was Christ," etc. And, similarly, it does not follow that "everything healthy is an animal; urine is healthy; therefore, urine is an animal," "a diet is healthy; therefore, a diet is an animate body," and so on and so forth. And, in general, when some term can be understood metaphorically and transumptively, it can cause the fallacy of equivocation. For example, in the following: "the subject of science is the matter of science; therefore, science is composed of matter and form"; for the antecedent of this consequence must be distinguished when the noun "matter" is interpreted properly [literally], and, therefore, "the subject of science is the matter of science" is false; or it can be understood metaphorically and improperly [figuratively], and therefore the consequence is invalid. Similarly, there is this: "a figure is a form of bronze; therefore, bronze and a figure are actually distinct"; for "form" can be taken properly, and the antecedent is therefore false, or it can be taken improperly and the consequent is therefore invalid. Similarly, there is this: "a statue is composed of bronze and a figure; therefore, bronze and a figure are actually distinct"; for "to be composed" can be taken properly, and the antecedent is therefore false, or metaphorically and improperly, and the consequent is therefore invalid.

And just as it is with those, so too is it with innumerable others, because there is scarcely any expression, especially [if] often used, that it is not sometimes understood metaphorically and improperly. And therefore, it is of utmost importance when examining the statements of authors to know when the words they use are meant properly and when improperly, because otherwise it is easy to be deceived. And on this account, ancient writers, because they excelled as much in the depth of their knowledge as in the splendor of their eloquence, found it necessary, for the sake of ornate discourse, to express their intention through different words and various forms of diction and speech, frequently shifting the sense of the words themselves from a proper to an improper [signification]. Grammarians discuss the various types of translation and metaphorical locution commonly used by authors, some of which occur when a word shifts from proper to improper signification, and these belong to the second mode of the fallacy of equivocation; but others occur when an expression shifts from proper to improper signification, but these belong to the fallacy of amphibology, some [examples] of which will be briefly touched on now.

One example is a shift that occurs when the name of a whole is posited for that of a part, or vice versa; for example, saying "this body is Socrates," indicating the cadaver that was a part of Socrates. Another is when one of [two] opposites is posited for the other. Another occurs when a cause is posited for the effect, or vice versa. Sometimes, too, a container is posited for the contents, or vice versa. And sometimes the name of the inventor is posited for the name of the invention, or vice versa. And sometimes the name of one species is posited for the name of another species, by reason of some property belonging to the individuals of both species. Sometimes the name of a manufactured product is posited for the name of the raw material, and vice versa. Sometimes the name of a time is posited for the effect of that time, and vice versa. Sometimes the name of antecedents for the name of consequents, and vice versa. And sometimes the name of a cause for the name of an effect, and vice versa. And sometimes a common name is appropriated by the particular. Sometimes a concrete name is posited for an abstract one, and vice versa. And sometimes the name of a human passion is attributed to God, and vice versa. And sometimes the verb of one tense is posited for the verb of another tense. And sometimes one case is posited for another case. And sometimes the quality of one part is attributed to another part or to the name of another part. Sometimes the singular is posited for the plural, and vice versa. And sometimes the quality of an animal is attributed to a non-animal, and vice versa. And sometimes one proposition is posited for another. And sometimes an expression of one part of speech is posited for that of another part of speech.

In these and many others ways, expressions can be shifted from proper to improper signification; grammarians teach the various types of these shiftings. Among which are the following: metaphor, synecdoche, metonymy, antonomasia, emphasis, catachresis, metalepsis, anthropopathism, onomatopoeia, phantasia, paralanguage, and many others, – the knowledge of which, in grammar, which ministers to all the sciences, [is] widely available to all those willing to learn from the books of authors and from Holy Scripture, [which] I believe very necessary, otherwise errors will frequently occur by perverting the intention of writers.

And note that such equivocation, according to the second mode [of equivocation], is called equivocation by design by Boethius.

Chapter 4: On the Third Mode of Equivocation

Regarding the third mode of equivocation, the first thing to understand is that it occurs, not when some term is taken for different significates, but only when it is compared to something that pertains no more to its primary signification than to its secondary one. And this mode does not occur because an utterance can signify different [things], as happens in the first two modes [of equivocation], but because the same utterance can supposit for different [things]. For this reason, various rules are given for this mode by which it can be recognized.

But there is one rule that, when one extreme of a proposition is a noun of primary intention, taken without a universal or particular sign, and the other extreme is a noun of secondary intention, – that proposition must be distinguished according to the third mode of equivocation, since the noun of first intention can supposit simply or personally, and for this reason the fallacy of equivocation can occur in the argument. And according to this [third] mode [of equivocation] such sophisms [as the following] are mistaken: "attributes are not the same as the divine essence; wisdom is an attribute, and similarly justice is an attribute; therefore, wisdom and justice are not the same as the divine essence." Response: the following proposition must be distinguished: "wisdom is an attribute," since "wisdom" can supposit either simply or personally. If taken simply, then it is [an instance of] the fallacy of equivocation, because in the minor [premise] "wisdom" is understood simply, but in the conclusion personally, and consequently it is equivocal. If taken personally, then the minor [premise] is false, because it does not denote that this concept which is attributed and concluded of God is an attribute, but that the thing that such a concept signifies is an attribute. Which is false because that thing which is divine wisdom is no more an attribute than that thing which is divine essence. And consequently, by accepting the terms personally and significatively,[4] this "wisdom is an attribute" is no truer than that "essence is an attribute." But by taking the terms simply and for the intentions of the soul, the one is true and the other false.

Similarly, it happens that "one is a passion[5] of being; one is actually the same as being; therefore, the same thing is a passion of itself." Similarly, there is this: "rational and man are actually the same thing; but rational is a differentia and man is a species; therefore, the species and its differentia are actually the same thing." Similarly, there is this: "man and risible are actually the same thing; but risible is a passion of man

---

[4]significatively. "A term is taken significatively if and only if it is taken for (supposits for) everything it primarily signifies." See Spade, Paul Vincent. *Thoughts, Words and Things: An Introduction to Late Mediaeval Logic and Semantic Theory.* Version 1.2: December 27, 2007.

[5]passion: from Latin *passio*, aka property, attribute. "A passion is something mental, spoken, or written that is predicable in the second mode of perseity of the subject whose passion it is said to be." Loux, Michael J., *Ockham's Theory of Terms, Part I of the Summa Logicae*, "On Passion," p. 121, University of Notre Dame Press, Indiana, 1974.

and man is the subject; therefore, the passion and its subject are actually the same thing."

The response to all this is clear: for these propositions – "one is a passion of being," "rational is a differentia of man," "risible is a passion of man," "man is the subject of risible," – are true only for subjects sup-positing simply. But other premises are true only for the same terms taken personally. And therefore, it is manifest in these [cases] that the fallacy of equivoca-tion according to the third mode is present.

Similarly, there is this: "man and a rational animal are really the same thing; man and a rational animal dif-fer in reason; therefore, some things which differ in reason are actually the same thing." Similarly, there is this: "wisdom and essence differ in reason, because they are distinct concepts; wisdom and essence are actually the same thing; therefore, some things which are actually the same thing differ in reason." Similar-ly, there is this: "man and a rational animal are actual-ly the same thing; man and a rational animal are a definition and the thing defined; therefore, a defini-tion and the thing defined are actually the same thing." Similarly, there is this: "man and an animal are the same thing; man is a species; animal is a genus; therefore, a genus and a species are the same thing."

Hence, in these [examples] and in countless consimi-lar ones, certain propositions can only be true when the terms are taken simply, and others can only be true when the same terms are taken personally. And thus it is patent that if the propositions are true, the terms are taken equivocally, and consequently they infer no conclusion.

Another rule is that when one extreme of a proposition is a noun of the first imposition, and the other extreme is a noun of the second, if the noun of the first is not taken with a universal or particular sign, the proposition must be distinguished, because the noun of the first imposition can be understood personally or materially.[6] Just as the proposition "man is a noun" must be distinguished because "man" can be understood personally and significatively, and thus is false, or [it can be understood] materially for that word, and thus it is true.

And thus sophisms such as the following are explained: "God and divine nature are actually the same thing; and God and divine nature are concrete and abstract; therefore, concrete and abstract things are actually the same thing." Response: "God and divine nature are concrete and abstract" must be distinguished since the terms "God" and "divine nature" can supposit materially, and thus the statement is true; and then they are understood equivocally in the major and minor [premises] and consequently infer no conclusion. Or they can supposit personally, and then the premise is false. In the same way, this argument is invalid: "man and risible are actually the same thing; man and risible are convertible[7] things; therefore con-

---

[6]first and second imposition: for a definition of these terms, see Loux, Michael J., *Ockham's Theory of Terms, Part I of the Summa Logicae*, "On Names of First and Second Imposition" and "On Names of First and Second Intention," pp. 72-73, University of Notre Dame Press, Indiana, 1974.

[7]convertible: interchangeable.

vertible things are actually the same thing." And it must be resolved in the same way.

Another rule can be given: that when a noun of first intention is compared to some common noun [refer-ring] specifically to intentions of the soul and to nouns of second imposition, that proposition [in which it is found] must be distinguished, because that noun can supposit simply or personally or materially, just as is clear in some of the aforementioned exam-ples. And these examples have been given merely by way of example. Such terms, common specifically to intentions of the soul and nouns of second imposition, are these: "universal," "common," "predicable," "sub-jectible," "noun" and many others of this sort.

It should also be known that the preceding rules are to be understood not only with respect to nouns but also with respect to every part of speech.

A fourth rule is this: when a common term supposits personally and is the subject of a verb in the preterite [tense], that proposition [in which it is found] must be distinguished, because the subject term can supposit for things that are, or things that were. For example, the following must be distinguished: "some boy was an old man," because "boy" can supposit for someone who is a boy, and then it is equivalent to this: "some-one, who presently is a boy, was an old man"; or it can supposit for someone who was a boy, and then it has the sense of "someone, who was a boy, was an old man." And by this distinction, sophisms such as the following are resolved: "something white was Socrates; therefore, Socrates was white," because if the subject of the antecedent stands for the things that are, the consequent is invalid; [but] if [it stands] for the things that were, the consequent is valid.

A fifth rule is this: when a common term, suppositing personally, is the subject of a verb in the future [tense], the proposition must be distinguished with respect to the third mode of equivocation, because the subject can supposit for the things that are or for the things that will be.

A sixth rule is this: when a common term, suppositing personally, is the subject with respect to a verb of possibility or contingency, the proposition must be distinguished, because the subject term can stand for the things that are, or for the things that can be, or for the things that happen to be.

Another rule is this: when the same word can be of various cases, genders, numbers, or other grammatical accidents, the proposition must be distinguished according to the third mode of equivocation. For example, this [proposition]: "those asses are bishops," [which must be distinguished] because "bishops" can be in the nominative case or in the genitive. However, in such a paralogism, the first mode of equivocation can frequently be assigned; but when this should and should not happen, I pass over for brevity's sake.

And it should be noted that this third mode of equivocation can be discovered in a purely mental proposition, although the first two modes [of equivocation] should not be involved except in signs established by convention. Hence, the mental proposition of "man is a species" can be distinguished, because the subject can supposit significatively or for itself [personally].

And the same must be said about similar [proposi-tions].

Chapter 5: On the Fallacy Amphibology

After the fallacy of equivocation comes the fallacy of amphibology. The first thing to know about it is that, just as the fallacy of equivocation occurs because a certain term can be understood in various ways, the fallacy of amphibology occurs because a certain statement can be understood in various ways, without, first, any term being understood in various ways; so that, just as a term can be ambiguous, so too can an entire statement.

The second thing to know is that, just as there are three modes of equivocation, so too are there three modes of amphibology. The first mode [of amphibology] is when a certain sentence, taken both primarily and properly *per se*, can have multiple significations. But when this occurs, there are different rules to be given for each of the different cases.

One rule, then, can be as follows: when [two] nouns in the same case are preceded by a verb that can govern both of them, and another verb in the infinitive [mood] is placed between them, the entire sentence is ambiguous and can have multiple significations. For instance, "I hear that the Greeks the Romans conquered";[8] because one sense is "I hear that the Romans conquered the Greeks" and another sense is "I

---

[8]"I hear that the Greeks the Romans conquered" obviously does not meet the requirements (in English). But it does in Latin, the original sentence being "audio Graecos vicisse Romanos."

hear that the Greeks conquered the Romans." And therefore, when a word can be of one case or another, it is not amphibology, as some say, but equivocation. But in the case where in every sense it is of the same case, it is amphibology, as in the example given.

Another rule is that a sentence in which the ablative absolute is employed is ambiguous according to amphibology, because such a proposition can be equivalent to a conditional, temporal, or causal [one]. For example, the following must be distinguished, "with no one running, horns grow on your forehead"; one sense is this: "if no one is running, horns grow on your forehead"; another sense is this: "because no one is running, horns grow on your forehead"; a third sense is this: "while no one is running, horns grow on your forehead." And each of them is false. Similarly, the following must be distinguished: "with no man existing, man is not an animal"; one sense is this: "if no man exists, man is not an animal." And that sense is true. Another sense is this: "because no man exists, man is not an animal." That sense is false. A third sense is this: "while no man exists, man is not an animal." Which, likewise, is false.

It must be noted that this same rule occurs when a gerundive is included in a proposition, as, for example, in the following: "having neither eye, you can see." For it has these meanings: "if you have neither eye, you can see"; "because you have neither eye, you can see"; "while you have neither eye, you can see." Another sense could be this: "although you had no eye, you could see," in other words, these two statements stand together: "you have no eye" and "you see."

From this it is clear that the following consequences are not valid: "with this man running, horns do not grow on your forehead; with that man running, horns do not grow on your forehead; and so on, for each particular case; therefore, with no man running, horns grow on your forehead"; "not having this eye, you can see; not having that eye, you can see; therefore, having neither eye, you can see," because just as hypotheticals cannot be inferred in such a way, neither can the equivalents to hypotheticals be inferred in such a way. Hence, just as the following is not valid: "if this man is running, horns do not grow on your forehead; if that man is running, horns do not grow on your forehead"; and so on, for each particular case; so too, this is not valid: "with this man running, horns do not grow on your forehead; and with that man running, horns do not grow on your forehead; etc., for each particular case; therefore, with no man running, horns...." And it must be said in the same way about similar things.

Another rule is this: when the dictum of an exclusive [term] is understood modally, the proposition must be distinguished because it can denote that the mode is verified of the entire exclusive [term] or it can denote that that mode is verified of the prejacent of an exclusive [term] and nothing else. In the first sense, the exclusive expression applies to the first subject of the prejacent [proposition]; in the second sense it makes an exclusion with respect to the entire prejacent. For example, the following must be distinguished with respect to amphibology: "that only a man is Socrates is true"; in the first sense it denotes "that only a man is Socrates" is true, and this sense is true. And thus it is clear that this word "only" exercises exclusion with respect to the subject "man." In the second sense it denotes that only this proposition is true: "a man is Socrates," and thus it exercises an exclusion with respect to the proposition "a man is Socrates," and it denotes that this proposition is true and no other.

The fourth rule is this: when a mode is taken with a dictum, the proposition must be distinguished, because the mode can be understood as applicable either to the entire proposition of which it is the dictum, or to an assertoric proposition in which either a demonstrative pronoun or proper noun supposits for something that the subject [also] supposits for with respect to the same predicate by means of the verb "is" in the present tense. For example, the following must be distinguished according to amphibology: "it happens that a silent person speaks"; one sense is this: "this is possible: a silent person speaks," and that sense is false. Another sense is this: "such a thing is possible: he speaks," referring to someone who is silent.

It must be understood that such propositions, which the two immediately-preceding rules address, are commonly distinguished by composition and division, a distinction that I frequently employ when speaking about them. That said, however, it happens that they can [also] be distinguished by amphibology. And it seems to me that it is easier to distinguish them according to amphibology than composition and division, because many [people] cannot see how, in such propositions, a mere change to a single punctuation mark, while preserving the same words in the same order, can produce different significations. But if such statements are distinguished by amphibology, their meanings are easily grasped following the method practiced by Boethius in his book *On Division*, in the interpretation of ambiguous sentences, because such interpretation is to be obtained either by addition or subtraction or division or some transmutation. And this method must be employed in such propositions, so that for this ambiguous statement: "it is possible for white to be black," the meanings to be determined are: "this is possible: white is black," "white can be black." And this clearly shows that in such statements, whether they are distinguished according to composition and division or according to amphibology, their meanings do not vary.

Secondly, it must be understood that the two aforementioned rules apply not only to the four famous modes, but also to all modes. Hence, all such [propositions] are to be distinguished: "that every man is an animal is known by you"; "that a white thing builds is *per se* true"; "that every triangle has three [sides], etc. is demonstrable," and so forth.

Thirdly, it must be understood that the last rule must be understood not only when a mode [modal expression] is included with the dictum of a proposition, but also when it is conjoined with a proposition by means of some verb and the word "that." Hence, all such [propositions] should be distinguished in the aforementioned manner: "I know that every man is an animal," "it is possible that a white thing be black," and so on, namely, such [statements] as "that any man be

Socrates, is possible," "that no white thing be a man, is necessary." For by the look of a proposition such as "it is possible that a white thing be black," one [person] may apprehend a meaning such as "this proposition is possible: white is black," [while] another [person] may understand a meaning such as "it is possible that something which is presently white could afterwards become black." And so, such propositions must be distinguished. And because such diverse meanings can be had without a difference in punctuation, amphibology exists in them, notwithstanding that there is composition and division.

Fourthly, it should be noted that to this mode the distinction of the following proposition has to be reduced "whoever says you are an animal, he says the truth," so that one sense of it may be this: "whoever proposes that 'you are an animal,' says the truth." And this sense is true. Another sense is this: "whoever states some proposition from which it follows that you are an animal, he says the truth." And this sense is false, because every proposition such as "you are an ass," "you are an ox," "you are a goat," and the like, implies this: "you are an animal," and yet, not everyone who says these things says the truth.

And if it be asked why such propositions must be distinguished, about which the aforesaid rules are given, it should be said that just as no reason can be given why some term is equivocal except the will of its users, so too no reason can be given why a statement is equivocal except the will of its users. And so, because different people conceive different meanings from such an uttered statement, therefore such a statement must be distinguished according to amphibology, according to Boethius' doctrine, in his book *On Division*, wherein he states: when ambiguous [statements are made,] each hearer reasonably believes that he has understood, so that when someone says "I hear that the Greeks the Romans conquered," one person may understand that the Greeks conquered the Romans, whereas another may understand it the other way around. So is it with such propositions, that when the following is uttered: "I know that every man is an animal," one person may understand "I know this proposition: every man is an animal," while another may understand "I know of each man that he is an animal."

The fifth rule is this: when the conjunction "or" is placed between two or more expressions, it must be distinguished because it may be disjunctive, in which case it divides propositions; or it may involve a disjunct extreme,[9] in which case it divides terms, and it is categorical. Hence, "every man is healthy or ill" should be distinguished in the same way, because one sense is this: "every man is healthy or every man is ill," which is false; another sense is this: "whatever man is referred to, he is either healthy or ill," which is true.

The sixth rule is this: when the conjunction "and" is placed between two terms, the proposition must be distinguished because it may be copulative or it may involve a copulative extreme. For example, this must be distinguished: "those there are Socrates and Plato," having indicated Socrates and Plato; one sense is this:

---

[9]extreme: the major or minor term in a syllogism.

"those there are Socrates and those there are Plato," and this sense is false; another sense is this: "those there are those men," and this sense is true.

The seventh rule is this: when the conjunction "if" is placed between two terms, the proposition must be distinguished because it may be conditional or it may involve a conditional extreme. For example, this must be distinguished, "every animal, if it is rational, is a man"; one sense is this: "if every animal is rational, every animal is a man," and this sense is true. Another sense is this: whatever this entire [phrase] is said about – "an animal, if it is rational" – the predicate "man" is said about it as well; and this sense is false, for the entire conditional "an animal, if it is rational" is predicated of an ass, and yet "man" is not predicated of an ass. And for this reason, sophisms such as the following can be resolved: "every truth, if it is necessary, is true; that you are an ass is true, if it is necessary; therefore, that you are an ass is true," because the major [premise] must be distinguished, in that it can be conditional, and therefore it is true, but the argument is invalid because from such a conditional and such a categorical, a categorical conclusion does not follow. Or it can be the major [premise] of a conditional subject, and in that case the consequence is valid, but the major [premise] is false.

The eighth rule is this: when the conjunction "because" is placed between two terms, it must be distinguished, because it may be causal or it may involve a causal extreme.

The ninth rule is this: when some temporal adverb is placed between two terms, the statement must be distinguished according to amphibology, because it may be temporal or it may involve a temporal extreme.

The tenth rule is this: when some adverb of place is placed between two terms, the statement must be distinguished according to amphibology, because it may be local or it may involve a local extreme.

It should be known that, according to many, the statements for which the six last rules are given must be distinguished according to composition and division; and whether what is said about them be true or false, it does not preclude their needing to be distinguished according to amphibology. And whatever might be said about that, I say that their distinction according to amphibology is clearer than the distinction according to composition and division, because it is difficult if not impossible in such [cases] to conceive of different meanings solely on account of a different punctuation of the same words spoken in the same order.

Secondly, it should be understood, for this [first] mode of amphibology, and for those that follow, that when assigning the different meanings of an ambiguous statement according to amphibology, those meanings must not be assigned under the same words, but under different ones, and by addition or subtraction or division or transmutation, as Boethius teaches in his book *On Division*. By addition, with respect to "I hear [that] the Trojans the Greeks conquered," the meaning can be ascribed as follows: "I hear [that] the Trojans conquered, and that the Greeks were conquered"; or "I hear [that] the Trojans were conquered, and that the Greeks conquered." By subtraction, thus: "I hear [that] the Greeks conquered." By division, thus: "The

Greeks conquered, the Trojans were conquered." By transmutation, thus: "I hear that the Greeks conquered the Trojans" or "I hear that the Trojans conquered the Greeks." And just as the meanings of the following ambiguous proposition – "I hear [that] the Greeks the Trojans conquered" – can be assigned to the different aforementioned modes, so too can other ambiguous statements according to amphibology [be assigned] to all or some of the aforementioned modes. And therefore, the multiple ambiguous meanings of the same statement are not always assigned to the same words, although different assignations may signify the same thing.

I mentioned Boethius earlier on account of some caviling that may be raised against some statements made here and against others made in various [other] opuscules of mine.

Moreover, besides these ten rules, many others could be given that pertain to the first mode of amphibology, which I pass over now for brevity's sake.

Chapter 6: On the Second Mode of Amphibology

Concerning the second mode of amphibology, it should be understood then that a statement is ambiguous with respect to the second mode when, properly and in its primary signification or imposition, it is understood in only one way, but [when] improperly and [in its] secondary [signification] it can be understood differently and have another sense. For example, the sentence "a wolf is in the fable" primarily and properly signifies that the fable is about a wolf, but improperly and secondarily it signifies that an enemy approaches. Similarly, the following statement "this [person] sells oil" primarily and properly signifies that this [person] sells such a liquid, but improperly and secondarily it signifies that this person fawns. And so, frequently, one statement is put for another, which, if they are properly understood, will have no agreement, neither in the significations of the terms nor in the significations of the complete statements.

And such a sense is not possible unless it is from the usage of speakers, putting one statement for another. This mode [of amphibology], however, frequently occurs, in Aristotle's opinion, in statements in which verbal nouns are employed, which according to the usage of many speakers do not supposit for the same [things] that participles do, or abstract [terms] formed from syncategorematic nouns, or from pronouns, adverbs, participles, conjunctions, prepositions, interjections, [or] many words joined together and in which an infinitive form of the verb is used in the place of a noun. Hence, all such propositions in which similar [expressions] occur can be distinguished since they can be taken uniformly for other statements composed of purely categorematic nouns and verbs, or they can be taken dissimilarly for other statements not having consimilar nouns. And so, the proposition "calefaction is in the agent" can be distinguished. One sense is that something distinct from the agent is in the agent, in the [same] way that, in the proposition "whiteness is in the white thing," one thing is denoted to exist in another, and so "calefaction is in the agent" is false. Another sense is this: "the agent is heated," so that the proposition "calefaction is in the agent" is substituted for "the agent is heated," and this is false; but under such a sense, "calefaction is in the thing heated" must be conceded. However, the proposition "calefaction is in the agent" can be understood differently, as standing for "the thing heating is the agent," and in that case it would be true.

Consimilarly, propositions such as the following must be distinguished: "motion is in the mobile thing." One sense of this is that "something brought about through motion, of which motion is verified, is in a mobile thing just as a distinct thing is in a distinct thing," and this is false in Aristotle's opinion. Another sense is this: "a mobile thing is moved," and this sense is true.

Consimilarly, this must be distinguished: "creation is in God." One sense is where a distinct thing is denoted to be in another [distinct thing]. Another sense is that "God creates."

Similarly, this must be distinguished, "The totality of

Socrates is in Socrates." One sense is that the totality is a thing existing in Socrates, the other sense is that Socrates is a certain totality.

Similarly, this is to be distinguished: "the haecceity of Socrates is something." One sense is that the haecceity, which is a thing distinct from others, is something; another sense is this: "Socrates, who is this man or this creature or this entity, is something."

Consimilarly, this must be distinguished: "negation is in the thing or from a part of the thing." One sense is that negation is something distinct from all other things and is a certain thing. Another sense is this: "something is truly negated by another thing," or this: just because a negative proposition is true does not mean [that] something exists in the nature of things; for example, just because this is true: "a man is not an ass," it does not follow that a man exists nor that an ass exists.

Similarly, this can be distinguished: "approximateness is something," so that one sense is this: "approximateness, which is not anything absolute, is something"; another sense is this: "something is related to something [else]."[10]

Similarly, the following proposition can be distinguished, if someone were to use such a proposition: "equanimity is something." One sense is that existence is denoted as being truly predicated of that for which the word "equanimity" supposits; another sense is this: "something exists, from which some-

---

[10]approximateness: the original Latin is *aditas*, which suggests a relation.

thing else exists."

Consimilarly is it [the case] with such [propositions as] "perseity is something." One sense is where "being" is predicated of something for which the noun "perseity" supposits; another sense is that a certain proposition is *per se*.

Similarly is [it the case] with this: "the necessity of a proposition is something." One sense is that something is verified about that which "the necessity of the proposition" supposits for; another sense is this: "some proposition is necessary." And consimilarly it is [the case] with all such [propositions].

However, it should be understood that, according to the usage of authors, such abstract [nouns] are frequently taken for concrete ones and vice versa.

Similarly, according to the opinion of some [authors], the following proposition must be distinguished: "God commits a sin," because it can be accepted properly, and consequently it denotes no more than that God does something that is a sin. And so they might concede, because they assert that some positive act is actually a sin, just as hating someone is a sin against the divine precept. On the other hand, this statement can be taken improperly, in their opinion, and then it is the equivalent of this: "God does something that he should not do" or this: "God sins," which is simply false. And the holders of that opinion would ascribe the fallacy of amphibology to this argument: this is a sin, indicating some sin of commission; God does this; therefore, God commits a sin. For they would say that the conclusion must be distin-

guished, because it can have many meanings. One
[sense] is this: "God does something, and that is a
sin," and they would concede this sense, and in doing
so they would concede the argument. Another sense
is this: "God does something that he ought not to do,"
and then the conclusion is false and the argument invalid. Just as it does not follow [that] "God does this;
and this is a sin; therefore, he does something that he
ought not to do," but rather it follows that he does
something that he himself or someone else ought not
to do.

Consimilarly, to the following argument they would
ascribe the fallacy of amphibology: "this is a sin; God
does not commit sins; therefore, God does not do
this," because they would distinguish the minor
premise just as before, and they would say in one
sense it is true and the argument valid, [while] in another sense they would say it is false and the argument invalid on account of the fallacy of amphibology.

And if it were said against them that, according to everyone, God does not commit sin, just as God does
not sin, they would respond that this [proposition]
"God sins" should be denied in every sense, and similarly for "God acts badly," "God does what He should
not do," and the like. And in place of such statements,
the Saints and others always use these expressions:
"God does not commit sin," "God does not do evil,"
which, however, according to them, can have one true
sense. And just as they would say about that, so too
would they say about this: "God intends evil." For
they would say that this has one true sense, namely,

that "God wants what is evil," in other words, "God wants something, and yet that thing is evil." But it has another, false sense, namely this: "God wants something that He ought not to want," or "God wants something evilly." Hence, this "God wants something evilly" is false in every way. And by doing so, they would attribute the fallacy of amphibology to this argument: "Whatever God conceives, he wants or can want; God conceives evil; therefore, God wants or can want evil," because the conclusion must be distinguished. One [possible] sense is this: "God wants or can want something that is evil," namely, that evil occurs because of something else, for instance because of a creature, and then they would concede the conclusion with that sense. Another sense is this: "God wants or can want something evilly," and then it is manifestly clear that the argument is invalid.

With respect to this second mode of amphibology, all propositions can be distinguished wherein the designated act is taken for the act performed or vice versa, because any such expression can be understood properly or improperly. Hence, this proposition: "the definition and the thing defined are the same thing" can be distinguished, because it can be understood properly, just as it sounds, and then it implies that the definition and the thing defined are not distinguished, but that the definition is the thing defined and vice versa. Alternatively, it can be understood improperly as in this proposition: "The definition and the thing defined imply the same thing or they are interchangeable," that is, they are predicated of each other interchangeably, and thus the proposition is true.

Similarly, this [proposition] can be distinguished: "certain things distinct in reason are one thing," because if it is taken properly, it is false; if improperly, expressly, it may be equivalent to this: "this predicate '[are] actually the same thing' is predicated of certain things having distinct definitions"; for example, "man" and "white," having distinct definitions, are predicated with this predicate: "[are] actually the same thing," which is equivalent to saying "'white' and 'man' are actually the same thing," and this is true.

Similarly, this [proposition] can be distinguished: "substance is predicated of a substance external to the soul." One sense is this: "a proposition is true when a substance external to the soul is made the subject and the substance is predicated," and then it is false. Another sense is this: "such a proposition is true: a substance external to the soul is a substance," where, however, the substance external to the soul is not the subject nor the predicate, but rather its sign.

Consimilarly, such [propositions] must be distinguished: color is the primary object of sight; man primarily is risible;[11] God under the aspect of divinity is a theological subject; a subject cannot exist without an attribute;[12] a species cannot exist without a genus, but conversely: a species is composed of a genus and a difference; the difference constitutes the species; a being is actually the same as its attributes [accidents]; the subject and the attribute are actually the same

---

[11]risible: scil., capable of laughing.

[12]attribute: The original word in Latin is "passion." Another way to translate attribute is quality, property, or accident.

thing; and innumerable propositions of this sort in logic and metaphysics must be distinguished. And similarly, in natural philosophy, according to the opinion of Aristotle, such propositions must be distinguished: there are only three principles of natural things; potentiality is corrupted by the advent of form; artificial things are distinguished from natural ones; bronze is the material [matter] of a statue; a statue is composed of bronze and form; motion is the act of a being in potentiality; motion and time differ; action and passion[13] are one motion; matter is subject to generation; something alterable is subject to alteration; a white thing builds *per accidens*; the potentialities of the soul are distinguished; the soul has multiple potentialities; and innumerable other propositions of this sort that Aristotle suggests, which, if they had been [made] explicit, would not have caused any difficulty, whereas now many people, reputed [to be] great, suffer great perplexity.

But these many grammatical tropes, often employed in sacred Scripture and in the books of the Saints and philosophers, belong to the second mode of amphibology. Namely, allegory, which contains seven species under it, which are: irony, antiphrasis, *charientismos*, enigma, paroemia [proverb], sarcasm, *astismos*. Likewise, homozeuxis, which has three species under it, which are: icon, parabola, and paradigm. Also, hypallage; and to this trope may be reduced all the expressions just now exemplified, and about which [more] will be said later. Also, hyperbole and hendiadys, to which many of those expressions can be reduced. And even other figures and tropes

---

[13]passion: or the thing acted upon (passively).

taught in grammar, which may belong to this fallacy, which it is up to the grammarian principally to discuss, and which I pass over now for brevity's sake.

But I do want to exemplify certain expressions often employed by theologians, and to declare in what way many pertain to this fallacy. Hence, I say that all such [propositions] as "God has justice," "God has wisdom," "God has intellect and [free] will," "God has essence," and all consimilar statements, in which a certain term is asserted denoting the distinction between what the subject supposits and [what] the predicate supposits, must be distinguished, in that they can be taken properly, and then they are false; or they can be taken improperly, so that in their place such [propositions] as "God is just," "God is wisdom," and so forth, are asserted, and then they are true. And Anselm[14] indicates the distinction of such [propositions] in his *Monologion*, chapter 16, wherein he maintains that it is improper to say that "supreme nature has justice," but rather that "justice exists." And so, while such propositions are frequently found in authoritative books, it is necessary that they be taken improperly.

And for the same reason, such expressions as "wisdom is in God," "justice is in God," "intelligence and volition are in God," and so forth, must be distinguished, in that they can be taken properly, and then they are false, because then they suggest some distinction between God and wisdom and between God and [His] volition and intelligence. If they are to be taken improperly, so that such propositions as "God is

---

[14]Anselm: Anselm of Canterbury (AD 1033-1109).

wisdom," "God is intelligence and volition," and so on, are understood through them, [then] they are true. And this distinction is indicated by St. Augustine in his book *De Trinitate* [On the Trinity], wherein he maintains that it is more proper to say "God is Wisdom" than "wisdom is in God."

And similarly, according to one opinion which posits that the divine persons are thoroughly indistinct from essence and relations, the following must be distinguished: "the Father has paternity," "paternity is constitutive of the Father," "filiation is a property of the Son," "essence and passive spiration constitute the Holy Spirit," and countless others, in that they can be accepted properly, and then they are false according to that opinion; in that their primary signification implies [that] the Father is distinguished from paternity and from essence, and the Son is distinguished from filiation. Because, if this was not implied, it could just as properly be said that the Father has paternity and that the Father constitutes the Father, as paternity constitutes the Father. By virtue of this discourse, therefore, such propositions seem false to the many who hold this opinion. Alternatively, such [propositions] can be understood improperly; for example, such phrases as "the Father is paternity," the Father is essence," "the Son is filiation," and so on; and in this way they are true. Hence, briefly, according to that opinion, every proposition by which, according to the propriety of expression, the Father is implied to be distinguished from essence and intellection and volition or wisdom or paternity, or the Son from the deity or filiation, or the Holy Spirit from essence or spiration, is false by virtue of the expression, although it could be true if taken improperly.

And if it were said against them that many such propositions are found in the books of the Saints who spoke properly, and therefore must be conceded according to the propriety of expression used, they might readily respond that such propositions are to be accepted in the sense in which they are made, not in the sense they make. And that they might be accepted as such can be demonstrated from the words of the Saints, as seen. For in other places they state that there is no distinction in the divine nature except among ingeneration, generation, and procession, and that the three persons are one essence, one deity, one wisdom. From which, and from many other [thing]s, it seems to many people that the intention of the Saints is that the Father is not distinguished by his paternity or by his essence. Nor does it seem inappropriate to say that the Saints frequently spoke improperly.[15] For the blessed Augustine asserts as much in his book *Confessions*, where he says that we say many things improperly, but few properly. And thus, opining in this way, they might say that all propositions that express some distinction between a divine person or persons and [their] essence or deity, or between persons and relations which are really [their] essence, are false according to the propriety of expression, although they are true if accepted according what the Saints have in mind. And consimilarly they might say that all such [propositions] are false according to the propriety of expression: divine volition and intellection are elicited operations; an elicited operation in divine nature presupposes a suppositum; the divine

---

[15]improperly: figuratively.

essence is, for the divine intellect, the foundation of understanding; the divine intellect understands its essence sooner than its creature; the essence exists before the production of the Son; the Father conceives the essence before he produces the Son; and many such propositions are false, although many of them could be explained for a proper understanding.

Likewise, a proposition such as "God, by his absolute power, can accept anyone without grace, but not by his ordained power" is ambiguous. One sense is that God by one power, which is absolute but not ordained, can accept someone without grace; but by a different power, which is ordained but not absolute, he cannot accept him, as if there were two powers in God, by one of which he could [do] it, and by the other he could not. And this sense is false. Otherwise, it is understood improperly [figuratively], as the following illustrates: God can accept someone without informing grace, because this does not involve a contradiction, and yet he has ordained that he will never do so. And this sense is true.

Similarly such propositions as: "a creature, as [it exists] in God, is the same as God"; "an ass, as [it exists] in God, is life"; "a stone, insofar as it exists in God, is eternal"; "a stone, in [its] objective being, is eternal," and suchlike propositions, must be distinguished, because if taken properly [literally], they are false, for a creature is in no way God, under any circumstances. For it is impossible that God and a creature should be one and the same thing. And it must be said analogously of other things. However, if they are understood improperly, as in the following: "the efficient cause of a creature is the same as God"; "the creative cause of an ass is life"; "the cognition by which God knows a stone is eternal"; "the cognition by which a stone is known by God is eternal," then they are all true. Hence, creatures do not exist in God except inasmuch as God knows them and is their author, as Peter Lombard states in *Magister Sententiarum*, Book I, Dist. 36, where, from his statements, it can be gathered that creatures do not exist in God, nor [do they exist] in some sort of quasi-intermediary state of divine cognition between God and God's cognition and those externally-produced creatures, as if initially there were God or God's cognition, then certain things somehow distinct, but actually the same as God, and afterwards the creatures were actually distinct from God, as many people imagine. But whatever is imaginable or can be or is God simply, and in no way a creature or in any way distinct from God, – is either a creature of God or can be, like the Antichrist, who admittedly is not a creature, but can be.

Similarly, a proposition such as "every attribute is actually identical with the divine essence" must be distinguished, because, if taken properly, it is false, since nothing is an attribute unless it is a predicable, which God is not; if [taken] improperly, it may be conceded, because what the attribute signifies is the divine essence. Similarly, propositions such as "whatever things are separable are not actually identical"; "when certain things are such that one of them can exist without the other, they are distinct" and so forth, [must be distinguished]; because they can be taken properly, and then they are true, because from the very fact that they are certain things, whether they be

separated or not, whether one of them can exist without the other or vice versa, they are distinct. Alternatively, they can be taken improperly for those propositions in which the predicate "to be separated" or
"are separated", taken significatively of certain terms
[also] taken significatively, can be verified in the
same way as "whiteness and sweetness are separated"
is verified to mean "not the same." When, however,
some terms are such that their existence can be verified of one [term] taken significatively, – that they exist to be truly negated of the other [term] taken significatively, – of those [terms] taken significatively, the
predicate of "not to be the same" or "to be distinct" is
verified. And then they are partially true and partially
false, because certain singular [propositions] are true
while certain others are false. For instance, the terms
"man" and "white man," since [the proposition] "a
man exists" may be true, while "a white man exists"
may be false; and, yet, this [proposition] is false: "a
man and a white man are distinct," or "a man and a
white man are not the same." But when all the terms
are merely absolute, such propositions contain truth;
nevertheless, any one of them, such as they are, is
possible, just as this is possible: "a man and a white
man are not the same."

Likewise, such propositions as "one potentiality has
diverse modes of operation," "diverse modes of being
can relate to the same thing without a variation in the
thing" and so on; because, if taken properly, understanding "mode" as something distinct from a thing,
such propositions are false. For when we say that the
soul, with respect to intellection and volition, has a
different mode of operation, we do not mean that

there are certain modes distinct from the soul and from the acts produced, as if they were some sort of intermediaries; for this is simply false, and therefore, under such an understanding, such propositions are false. Another sense is this: "the same thing acts in different ways," for instance, it necessarily elicits intellection and contingently and freely elicits volition.

Similarly, if it is said that another mode of being belongs to the body of Christ in heaven and in the Sacrament of the Altar, it must not be imagined that the mode of being that belongs to the body of Christ in heaven is something adding to the body of Christ, distinct from something else adding to the body of Christ in the Sacrament. But we do not understand by such a proposition anything other than that the body of Christ is circumscriptively in a place in heaven and not in the Sacrament of the Altar.

And if you asked what that circumscription is, I would tell you that it is a meaningless word, just like "bu-ba." Hence, to invent such abstractions from such adverbs, verbs, prepositions, and the like, is the occasion of many errors for simpletons; nevertheless, it can sometimes be useful for intelligent people, in that by such fictions they can frequently speak more briefly.

Likewise, every statement in which the infinitive mood is used for the suppositum [or subject], as in, for example, "to read is good," "to run is to be moved," "to heat is to act," and the like, can be distinguished, because one sense can be [that] by which the predicate is seen to apply to something that is neither the agent, nor patient, nor effect, as if such infinitive moods introduced something distinct from the agent, patient, and effect, and other such like things which can be the agent, patient and effect of the thing produced. And such a sense is simply false according to Aristotle's principles. Another sense can be that such propositions are substituted for statements in which the participle is predicated of a participle or a verb of the participle or two corresponding verbs of the same [subject], so that a statement like "to heat is to act" has the sense of "that which heats, acts" or "heating is acting"; and "to read is good" has the same sense as "he who reads does good work" or "he who reads does good" and so on. And in this way many difficulties are avoided.

Likewise, hypothetical propositions must frequently be distinguished, because authors often substitute one for another, as when a temporal [clause] is substituted for a conditional one; for example, "everything that exists, when it exists, must needs exist." For this, by virtue of the way it is expressed, is temporal, but it is substituted for the conditional statement "if something exists, it exists," which is necessar[il]y [true]. And so it is with many [propositions]. And these examples of [the second mode of] amphibology should suffice for now, for brevity's sake.

About this second mode [of amphibology], it should also be understood that no fixed rule can be given by which one might regularly and sufficiently determine whether amphibology is involved or not, because it depends entirely on the will and usage of speakers, just as with the second mode of equivocation.

Chapter 7: On the Third Mode of Amphibology

The third mode of amphibology is when a statement, taken by itself, has only one meaning, whereas when it is joined with other statements it can have multiple meanings.

Or, because of insistent people, it can be said that the third mode of amphibology is when a statement taken by itself lacks any sense, which it can acquire, however, from conjunction with another statement. For example, the proposition "the world knows" has only one sense, namely, that the world knows something; yet if the proposition "Plato sees Socrates" were preposed, so that it were said that "Plato sees Socrates and knows the world," it can have another sense, which is that "Plato has knowledge of the world."

It must be understood, however, that this mode [of amphibology] frequently occurs in statements containing a relative pronoun. For sometimes the pronoun included in a statement, with no other addition to it, can only be demonstrative, but if some statement preceded [it], it can be relative, as in the case of the pronoun "that." Hence, this "she saved" need not be distinguished according to amphibology; but if the proposition "the woman damned" preceded it, so that the text read "the woman damned and she saved," then it must be distinguished according to the [third] mode [of amphibology] in that it can be a personal relation or a simple one, as per the grammarians – in other words, because the [pronoun] can refer to either the same number[16] or the same species in the antecedent. In the first sense, it is false; in the second, it is true.

It should also be understood that the ambiguity may result from [the use of] a relative [pronoun], in that it can refer to the same number or same species [in the antecedent]; but sometimes the relation pertains to the signification; other times only to the expression. And the statements "a white man is a man and he differs in reason from a man" can be distinguished according to this mode [of amphibology], for if the relation refers to a expression or a concept, it is true, but if to the thing signified, it is false.

And similarly, just as such propositions involving the relative [pronoun] "that" can be distinguished, so too can many propositions involving the relative pronoun "who." But whether this distinction be according to equivocation or amphibology and, if according to amphibology, according to which mode they must be distinguished, I omit to discuss for brevity's sake. Nevertheless, for now it should suffice to know that such propositions [as] "certain things that differ in reason are actually the same" must be distinguished.[17] One sense is this: "certain things differ in reason, and those things are actually the same in number," and this sense is false, since things that differ in reason

---

[16]number: individual

[17]differ in reason: things that differ in reason are things that have different concepts (or intentions) in the mind, but which may refer to the same thing in reality (in re). Consequently, they may need to be distinguished.

are either different definables or different reasons, but neither different definables nor different reasons are one [and the same] thing. Another sense is this: "certain things differ in reason, and yet, of those [things] taken significatively, it is predicated [that they] are actually the same," or "that which is meant by each of them, and for which each of them supposits, is actually the same thing," and thus what is referred to is the thing [itself], and not to the sign. But in the [proposition] "some things are actually the same, which differ in reason," in the sense in which it is true, a reference is made to terms or signs, as in the proposition "God gives a halo, which is made of gold." Thus, the following [propositions] could be distinguished: "man is musical, which is said from [the perspective of] music."

And just as such propositions can be distinguished where the relative [pronoun] "which" is used, so too can [such] propositions be distinguished where, in the second clause, the relative pronoun is suppressed but implied, such as: "a man and a white man are actually the same but differ in reason"; "matter and privation are one in number and differ in reason;" "subject and predicate are one in number and differ in reason"; "intellect and will are actually the same [thing] and differ in reason;" and many consimilar [propositions] are to be distinguished with respect to amphibology. And generally [speaking], any statement about which different [people] come away with different meanings – where the difference in meanings does not arise from a precise word included in a statement, nor from a different punctuation of the same words in the same order, nor from a [different] accent [stress] – must be distinguished with respect to amphibology, and this according to the first, second, or third mode.

If it were said that the ambiguity in this statement "Socrates and white Socrates are really the same and they differ in reason" arose from the word "they," then this would be equivocation; similarly, [if] the ambiguity in [this statement] "some things which are really the same are distinguished in reason" arose from the word "which," then it is [also] equivocation, and not amphibology.

It must be said, however, that it is not a great concern for now whether equivocation or amphibology be ascribed to it, since both perhaps could be ascribed to it, nor is it unheard of for these two fallacies to coincide. Hence, in the first [case] there is amphibology inasmuch as there is no ambiguity unless one statement is conjoined with another. In the second, however, there is amphibology in that a diversity of meanings arises from the fact that the same statement can be expressed by different statements, although that [alone] may not be sufficient for the ambiguity of amphibology.

It can be said, however, that in such [cases] the second mode of amphibology is involved because it is precisely through such statements that it is conveyed that those very same things and not others, which differ in reason, are one and the same thing. Which is impossible. However, it is improperly conveyed by the fact that those very same things which have distinct definitions are verified of the same thing, for the same thing, not for themselves, however, but rather for the same thing that they signify; just as the terms "white" and "musical" have different definitions expressing the nominal definition,[18] and yet they signify the same man and supposit for the same man, as for example in "the white [man] is musical." And, thus, those [things] which are distinguished in reason are terms, but that which is really the same is something conveyed by the term. Which is no different than saying that the signs are distinct and the signification is the same.[19]

---

[18]nominal definition: *quid nominis*.

[19]In other words, things that "differ in reason" have different intentions (or concepts) in the mind, but they may refer to the same thing in reality (*in re*). If they refer to the same thing, then they may need distinguishing.

Chapter 8. On the Fallacy of Composition and Division

After the foregoing, [the fallacy of] composition and division must be discussed. And it must first be known, then, that a certain statement is [considered] complex[20] according to composition and division when, spoken or written, it can have different meanings based solely on variations in punctuation. For example, this statement: "whatever lives always exists," if it were punctuated as "whatever lives always, exists" has one sense, but if it were punctuated as "whatever lives, always exists" has another sense. So that the reason for the appearance of this fallacy is the identity of the same words in the composite and divided statement, [and] the reason for its non-existence is the difference in punctuation.

There are two principal modes of this fallacy. The first is when the entire statement, whether it be composite or divided, remains either categorical or hypothetical in sense. The second is when a composite proposition is categorical in sense and a divided one hypothetical. And according to this a distinction could be made between composition and division, such that those statements are said [to be] multiple [in meaning][21] according to composition when each proposi-

---

[20]complex: ambiguous, having multiple meanings.

[21]multiple [in meaning]: i.e., ambiguous.

tion is categorical in sense or each is hypothetical; and those are said [to be] multiple [in meaning] according to division when one proposition is categorical in sense and the other is hypothetical. However, I am not particularly concerned whether the distinction of these fallacies should be taken in this way, because I do not consider knowing this to be useful to specific sciences [or knowledge domains], even though the notion of being able to distinguish such statements has great utility.

According to the first mode, here are some examples of statements of multiple meaning, which the Philosopher posits in his book *On Sophistical Refutations*: "it is possible [for someone] seated to walk," and "it is possible [for someone] not writing to write"; for if it were said that "it is possible, [for someone] seated, to walk" and "it is possible, [for someone] not writing, to write," they are true, because they denote that someone who is seated now can walk now or later, and that someone who is not writing now can write now or later, which are true. Alternatively, they can be punctuated as follows: "it is possible, [for someone] seated to walk," "it is possible, [for someone] not writing to write"; and then it is implied that it is possible that someone [who is] not writing might be writing; and that someone [who is] seated might be walking; and as such they are false. And in this same way they can be distinguished, all propositions in which a certain modality is posited with the dictum of the proposition, although they can also be distinguished according to amphibology.

And it seems to me that they can be distinguished according to amphibology more clearly and plainly in the Latin language, although perhaps, in the idiom of Aristotle or in the Greek language, the multiplicity of such statements might be more plain[ly distinguished] according to composition and division than according to amphibology. But whether they should be distinguished according to one fallacy or another, I say that the meanings do not vary.

Hence, statements of multiplicity such as "it is possible for the suppositum to be assumed by the Word" have to be distinguished. One sense is where it is denoted that something that is now a suppositum can now or later be assumed by the Word. And this is true, because that nature which presently is a complete intellectual nature and is neither multiple supposita nor sustained by another suppositum, and consequently is a suppositum, can afterwards be assumed, just as it can be sustained by another suppositum. Another sense is where it is denoted that it is possible that something might simultaneously be a suppositum and assumed by the Word. Which is impossible, just as this is impossible: "some suppositum is assumed by the Word."

Similarly, this must be distinguished: "it is possible for a quantitative substance not to be a quantity." One sense is this: "it is possible for a quantitative substance, while it is quantitative, not to be a quantity," and the sense is false according to the opinion that says that a quantitative substance is a quantity. Another sense is this: "it is possible that a substance which is quantitative now not be a quantity later," and this sense is true.

Similarly, this must be distinguished: "it is possible for this man not to be God," indicating the Christ. One sense is where it is implied that it is possible for the statement "this man is not God" to be true, and this is true because it is possible. For if the Son of God were to renounce human nature, [then] this [statement] would be true: "this man is not God," because the following would be true: "he is not man." Another sense is one in which it is implied that is possible that he who is now man may afterwards not be God. And this is impossible, because the Son of God who is now man will always and necessarily be God.

And consimilarly such propositions must be distinguished: "it is possible for the creator not to be God," "it is possible for the predestined to be damned," "it is possible for the foreknown to be saved," "it is possible for what is true to be impossible." Similarly, such [propositions as]: "it is true that a white thing builds *per se*," "it is necessary for a man to be God," "it is necessary for the creator to be God," and so forth. And in what sense they are true, and in what sense false, can be made clear from what has preceded.

Similarly, many statements must be distinguished because one word can be joined with one or another [word]; for example "what someone knows now he learned," because the adverb "now" can qualify knows, so that the sense is "what someone knows now, he learned," and this sense is true, because what he knows now, he learned at one time [in the past]. Or it can qualify the verb "learned," so that the sense is "what someone knows, now he learned," and this sense is false. It is similarly [the case] with the following statements given by the Philosopher: "I made you, being a slave, free"; "the wealthy Achilles abandoned forty men out of a hundred." Likewise, such statements as the Philosopher made, which, although he does not explicitly say so, he supposes that they must be distinguished: "you saw [that man] struck with a stick," "you saw the striking with your eyes."

Similarly, as often [happens], statements in which an adjective is placed together with a substantive must be distinguished, for example: "he is a good cobbler," while pointing out a bad man. If the statement is divided, it is false, because then what is meant is that he is good and that he is a cobbler; but if it is composite, then the statement is true because what is meant is that he has perfectly [mastered] the art of cobbling [but he is a bad person]. And although such statements can be distinguished according to composition and division, nevertheless it seems to me that they can also be distinguished according to amphibology, and the meanings will not vary. Similarly, such propositions as "he is a white monk" can be distinguished; in one sense it means that he is white and that he is a monk, in another sense it means that he is a monk by profession.[22]

As for the second mode, there are propositions that must be distinguished in which words making hypothetical propositions are placed between two terms, and in one sense it will be a categorical proposition, and in another sense it will be a hypothetical one. And in the same way, as was said earlier, they [the propositions] are distinguished according to the falla-

---

[22]white monk: a member of the Order of Cistercians.

cy of amphibology. Hence, this [statement] must be distinguished: "five are two and three" because in one sense it means that five are two and that five are three, in another sense it means that five are these, indicated as two and three. Similarly this must be distinguished: "he can carry one stone and another"; in one sense it means that he can carry one stone and that he can carry another stone, and the sense is one of division; in another sense it means that he can carry this stone and that one at the same time.

So the following proposition must be distinguished which is a premise in a paralogism that ends with this conclusion: "because he can carry one, he can carry many." Which is not to be distinguished according to composition and division, but can be distinguished according to amphibology, because one sense may be this: "whoever can carry one stone, although he does not carry more, can carry more," and this is true; another sense is this: "whoever can carry one stone but not more, can carry more," and this sense is false. And this is amphibology, just as this [is]: "every man is only one man," because one sense is this: "every man is one man, and there are not more men than one"; another sense is "every man is one man, and no man is many men."

Similarly, this must be distinguished: "only one [man] exists."

Chapter 9. On the Fallacy of Accent

With respect to the fallacy of accent, the first thing to be understood is that deception occurs as a result of the fallacy of accent when the same utterance made with different accents signifies different things. And this can happen in three ways. In one way because some syllable of the same word can have different accents; in another way because the same word can be pronounced with or without aspiration; in a third way because the same utterance can be either a word or a statement.

The first way is more apt to deceive in writing than in speech, because such a word is written in only one way, but it is uttered in different ways. And in this way the statement "it is good for just men to *pendere*" must be distinguished because the middle syllable of the word *pendere* in Latin can be made short or long.[23]

The second way never deceives in writing, but only in speech, because in writing the aspiration must be indicated clearly and sensibly, or not at all. In speech, however, it is sometimes neither clearly nor easily discerned whether the word is spoken with or without aspiration.

The third way can deceive as much in writing as in speech. And according to this way, such a statement

---

[23]*pendere*: to ponder or consider; but *pendēre*: to hang or be suspended.

must be distinguished: "God makes the fronds and leaves *invite*," because *invite*[24] (unwillingly) can be one word, that is, an adverb, and then it is false, given it signifies that God makes something under coercion; or it can be two words, that is, the preposition *in* and the ablative case of the noun *vitis* (in the vine) and then is it true.

Regarding this fallacy there are no great difficulties in the particular sciences [knowledge domains], and therefore what has just been said about this fallacy should suffice.

---

[24]*vitis*: For this to make any sense, one needs to realize that the word in Latin, *invite*, has two meanings: one is "unwillingly" (where the first "i" in *invīte* is short and the second long); the other is "in the vine" (where the first "i" in *īnvite* is long and the second short).

Chapter 10. On the Fallacy of Figure of Speech

After the fallacies in diction, according to which certain terms (or utterances) are ambiguous, the fallacy of figure of speech must be discussed, which does not arise from an ambiguous statement, but rather from the similarity of certain words. So that the fallacy of figure of speech is a deception originating from the similarity of certain words; the reason for its appearance is the similarity of one word to another, and the reason for its non-existence is the difference in significations, or modes of signifying, or the grammatical accidents of the words. And I take "significations" in the broadest sense of the word.

Hence, the general method for solving paralogisms involving this fallacy is to clarify any difference in significations, or modes of signifying, or the [grammatical] accidents of words that invalidate the argument. For this fallacy always occurs when, because a certain mode of arguing holds [valid] for some words, it is believed that such a mode of arguing holds for other consimilar words, in which, however, it does not, because the words are different; although they may seem similar, they have different significations (taking "significations" in the broadest sense of the word), or a different mode of signifying, or different grammatical accidents. For example, we see that this syllogism is valid: "every corporeal substance is colored; a goat is a corporeal substance; therefore, a goat is colored," such that there is no variation between the predicate of the major premise and that of the conclusion. If, on this account, it is believed that, in a consimilar manner of arguing, with the exception of certain terms, there should be no variation made between the predicate of the major premise and that of the conclusion, as in the following argument: "every corporeal substance is colored; a patriarch is a corporeal substance; therefore a patriarch is colored,"[25] then a deception arises through the fallacy of figure of speech.

Hence, in general, whenever there is the fallacy of figure of speech, it is possible to find a similar mode of valid argumentation using other terms, and this is on account of a difference in grammatical accidents, or in modes of signifying, or on account of a difference in significations, while taking "significations" in the broadest sense of the word.

According to what has been said, three modes of this fallacy may be understood. The first of which occurs when there is a defect in reasoning due to a difference in the grammatical accidents of various words. And such a sophistical mode of arguing always or frequently leads to solecism. Hence, if one should argue in this way: "every animal is colored; man is an animal; therefore man is colored," it must be said that

---

[25] a patriarch is colored: in Latin it is "patriarcha est colorata," where "patriarcha" is a singular masculine noun (in the nominative case), and colorata is singular feminine form of the adjective (in the nominative case). The mismatch, and therefore the fallacy, occurs because of a mismatch in genders. In English we cannot see it, and it does not exist, but in Latin it we can and it does, because of the "grammatical accident of words."

this is [an instance of] the fallacy of figure of speech. Indeed, because the word *homo* [man] is not of the neuter gender as "animal" is, then "man is a colored thing" is not the conclusion that should be inferred, but rather "man is colored."[26] And sometimes the variation of a vowel in some term must be made in different propositions to account for the variation in accidents of the different terms.

Similarly, the following [syllogism] can be ascribed to the fallacy of figure of speech: "every white thing is a body; every man is a white thing; therefore, every man is a body."

And if it is said that in every fallacy there must always be a certain appearance [of the truth], but none is seen here, therefore, etc. it must be said that it is not required for every fallacy to have as much appearance as may deceive the wise, but only so much as might beguile simpletons. And so it is in the case at hand, because some simpletons may be deceived by such statements.

The second principal mode of this fallacy is understood from the different significations of various words. Nevertheless, a certain sort of difference in some manner of arguing is sufficient for this fallacy, but another sort is not. Knowing when exactly it suffices and when it does not, however, cannot be known through logic, just as logic is not especially helpful in determining, for any given word, whether such a word is equivocal or not; this must be [obtained] by special sciences [domains of knowledge].

---

[26]a man is a colored thing: vs. man is colored. In Latin, the difference is revealed by gender: "coloratum" vs. "coloratus."

In this mode, sophistical arguments such as "to heat is to act; therefore, to see is to act" and "to be heated is to suffer; therefore, to be seen is to suffer" are erroneous. The appearance of these sophistical consequences is due to the similar verb endings: "to see – to heat," "to be seen – to be heated."

Their non-existence (or non-appearance) is due to a difference in significations. Indeed, since "to heat" signifies heat caused by a heater in the heated object, and "to see" signifies vision caused by an object seen in the seer, and is not caused by a seer in the object seen, therefore the consequence does not follow.

Similarly, such logical consequences as "the heater is an agent, therefore the seer is an agent" and "the heated object suffers, therefore the seen object suffers" are invalid. And in general, when words have the same grammatical accidents and the same modes of signifying, and on account of this they have consimilar endings and consimilar modes of signifying, it is believed that the common predicable that is verified of one thing should be verified of the other; and yet, because the things they signify differ, it is not so; but rather it is [an instance of] the fallacy of figure of speech. And this mode of the fallacy of figure of speech often occurs when one argues by analogy or similarly. For example: since "seen" is a passive participle, according to grammarians, it may be believed that just as "heated," also a passive participle, can only be verified of the object passively acted on, so too is it with "seen." And by believing in this way, by being ignorant of the nature of signification through these terms, or by being ignorant of what they signify and how, one is deceived by the fallacy of figure of speech. For if someone believed that just as "heated" signifies what receives heat and that in which the heat resides nominatively, and that by which it receives the heat obliquely, so too "seen" might signify that in which sight resides nominatively, and that by which it is seen obliquely – he would be deceived. And therefore, in order to understand this mode of [the fallacy of] figure of speech fully, it is necessary to know the natures of things, as well as the grammar by which one knows what a word signifies in one way of signifying and in another. And yet, this mode is due not to a difference in the way certain words signify, – since, to be sure, one word has one way of signifying and another word has another way – but it is due rather to a difference in significations. Because different things are signified by the term "seen" and by the term "heated," although they employ the same modes of signifying, there is this fallacy.

It must be understood, however, that this mode does not occur only when, on account of consimilar endings and consimilar modes of signifying, it is believed that what is common to one is common to another, – just as when someone argues that "white is a quality; therefore, a sea swallow is a quality"; "quality actually differs from substance; therefore, quantity actually differs from substance"; "music belongs to the feminine gender; therefore, prophet belongs to the feminine gender," etc., etc. – but this mode can also occur when, on account of the nature of the thing signified, some discourse or consequence is valid which would not be valid [if another] term [were] substituted for the one [already] placed there. For example, according to Aristotle, this is a valid argument: "he will give a colored ox; he does not have a colored ox; therefore, he will give an ox that he does not have"; but arguing like this: "he will give a white ox; he does not have a white ox; therefore, he will give an ox that he does not have" is not valid because [although] the premises may be true, the conclusion is false.

Similarly, the following discourse is valid: "he is now white; he will not be white tomorrow; therefore, he will give up something that he now has." And yet the following discourse, according to Aristotle's principles, is not valid: "this air is now two cubits; this air will not be two cubits tomorrow; therefore, this air will lose something tomorrow that it now has." And yet the same mode of reasoning is seen in both instances. Therefore, if someone believes that because a certain mode of reasoning holds in one instance, it will hold in all instances, [then] he is deceived by the fallacy of figure of speech.

And if it were asked why the fallacy of figure of speech occurs more in one argument than in another, it must be said that this is because the intrinsic medium[27] by which one argument holds is necessary, whereas the intrinsic medium by which the other holds is not.

To clarify, it must be understood that certain consequences, even formal ones, hold by means of the intrinsic medium, whereas certain others hold by means

[27]intrinsic medium: *medium intrinsecum*: "a proposition formed from terms contained in the *consequentia*." See "Consequentiae" in *The Development of Logic*, Kneale, William and Martha. Oxford University Press, 1962.

of the extrinsic medium.[28] Those that hold by means of the intrinsic medium do so by virtue of a single proposition formed from the same terms; just as the consequence "every man is an animal; therefore, Socrates is an animal" holds by means of the intrinsic medium because it holds by virtue of a single proposition formed from the same terms, namely, from the terms "Socrates" and "man," – since it holds by virtue of this medium: "Socrates is a man." For if this proposition were false, the first consequence would not be valid at all. However, those consequences or arguments hold by means of the extrinsic medium; they hold sufficiently by virtue of some general rule not formed from the terms of such a consequence or argument, – or if it is formed from them, it is [formed] accidentally, because other consequences and arguments hold just as well by this medium or by such an extrinsic medium from whose terms such a general rule is not formed. This is clear from the following consequence: "every man is an animal; therefore, only an animal is a man," which holds by means of this medium [rule]: "a good consequent results when the terms are transposed from the universal to the exclusive." And the consequence "every man is an animal; therefore, some animal is a man" holds by the rule that "the universal affirmative[29] is converted *per accidens*." And, therefore, whenever some consequences or arguments are observed which are not cor-

---

[28]extrinsic medium: *medium extrinsecum*: "a general rule which is no more concerned with the terms of the *consequentia* than with any others." Ibid.

[29]universal affirmative: one of the four primary categorical propositions identified by Aristotle.

rected or governed by some general rule, it must be seen whether they might be corrected by some true proposition formed from the same terms.

And if so, the consequence will be valid; if not, the consequence will be invalid. And so it is in this case. For consequences such as "the man does not have a colored ox; the man will give a colored ox; therefore, he will give an ox that he does not have" and "the man will give a white ox; the man does not have a white ox; therefore, the man will give an ox that he does not have" cannot be corrected by any general rule; therefore, if they are valid, there must be some true medium [formed] from the same terms. And so it is here that the first consequence holds by means of the true and necessary medium, according to Aristotle's principle, which is this: "if something is an ox, it itself is a colored ox."

Hence, because according to Aristotle's principle it is impossible that something should be an ox and not be colored, therefore, this consequence is valid: "he will give a colored ox; and he does not have a colored ox; therefore, he will give an ox that he does not have." But because it is possible for the same individual ox not to be white at first, but to be white later, then the intrinsic medium by which another consequence holds – "if something is an ox, it itself is white" – is simply false. And therefore, the following argument is not valid: "he will give a white ox; he does not have a white ox; therefore, he will give an ox that he does not have," because he will be able to give an ox that he has, which now is not white, but which may be white when he gives it.

Similarly, the following consequence is valid: "he is white now; he will not be white tomorrow; therefore, he will be lacking something that he now has," and it holds by virtue of this medium: "whiteness signifies something totally distinct in itself from that which is white." But, according to Aristotle's principles, the following consequence is not valid: "this air is now two cubits; this air, tomorrow, will not be two cubits; therefore, this air will lack something that it now has," because, according to Aristotle's principles, the following is false: "two cubits signifies something totally distinct in itself from that which is two cubits and from that which is a part of it." And so, in general, when a consequence holds in certain terms by virtue of a necessary intrinsic medium, – and another consequence whose terms have consimilar modes of signification, although they may not signify the same things in the same way as other terms signify them or other things, is invalid because of the absence of such an intrinsic medium, – this can be assigned to the fallacy of figure of speech. Hence, here is [an example of] the fallacy of figure of speech: "he is a father; he was not a father; therefore, he has changed," or "he is similar; he will not be similar; therefore, he will be changed," and so forth.

But it should be known that this mode of the fallacy of figure of speech never occurs when two premises that are purely categorical, purely assertoric, and purely in the present [tense], are arranged verbally in mood and figure.[30] And therefore, this mode of arguing from some proposition in the past or future

---

[30]mood and figure: according to Aristotle's definition of syllogistic logic rules. See also Spade.

[tense], or of a certain modality,[31] often occurs. Hence, the following is [an instance of] the fallacy of figure of speech: "he can be white; he is not white; therefore, he can be something that now he is not." Similarly this: "The Son of God was not a man from eternity; the Son of God was a man in time; therefore, the Son of God was something in time that was not from eternity."

Nevertheless, in these [cases], not just this mode can be assigned, but also the third mode, about which more will be said immediately hereafter, as will be clear in the same place.

The third principle mode [of the fallacy] of figure of speech arises from a diversity of modes of significa-tion in the various expressions that seem similar [but are not], on account of which one is sometimes de-ceived into believing that they must be reasoned about in the same way. And this mode can be subdi-vided.

To understand this, it [should be] known that modes of signification are not some things added to the ex-pressions themselves, coming into them,[32] instead, it is a metaphorical way of speaking to say that the ex-pressions have different modes of signifying, because by such a statement the following statement is under-stood: "different words signify what they signify in

[31]modality: see chapter 33, "On Signification" in Book 1 of *Summa Logicae*: "a sign signifies something when it is capable of suppositing for that thing in a true past, present, or future proposition or in a true modal proposition."

[32]coming into them: scil. predicated of them. See chapter 32, "On Inherence and Being In" in Book 1, "On Terms."

different ways." Because some expressions do not have proper signification, but rather, conjoined to others, they consignify, or allow other expressions to supposit, or stand in a determinate way – in any case, they are syncategorematic, namely conjunctions, prepositions, and the like. But some [expressions] signify determinately and with finite signification, according to Boethius' manner of speaking, for example categorematic nouns and pronouns and participles and the like; and, of these, a certain [number] are purely absolute nouns and certain [others are] connotative, as was said in the first treatise.

Similarly, certain [expressions] are proper, like pronouns and proper nouns, while others are common, which therefore have a different mode of signification because the one signifies one thing and not many, while the other signifies, or can signify, many.

And, as mentioned earlier, under this third principal mode are grouped three special [sub]modes of this fallacy. The first mode can be described as expressions that have finite significations and those that do not. And according to this mode, the consequents in which one mode of supposition is commuted into another are in error; just as in this argument: "every man is an animal; therefore, an animal is every man."

And in support of this example and [those] like it, it should first be understood that in this case the fallacy of figure of speech can be ascribed [to it] because the same expression has one supposition in the antecedent and it has another in the consequent, although this may not be sufficient, as will be shown. And the similarity of expressions is the reason for this deception; for in many [cases] transposing the words makes no difference – for example, the following [proposition]: "a white man is a man; therefore, a man is a white man," which is similar to this one: "a rational animal is a man; therefore, a man is a rational animal" – on account of which someone could be deceived into believing that such a way of arguing is always valid, and he would be deceived by the fallacy of figure of speech. And this fallacy arises from a diversity of modes of signification. On account of which, the word "every" does not have the same mode of signification as "white" or a similar word, but only consignifies or makes the term to which it is added stand for all its significata, and it makes the mediately following term stand merely confusedly, as it does not stand in the consequent, therefore it is a fallacy of figure of speech and it arises from the similarity of one expression to another.

And it should be known that not [just] any variation in supposition causes a fallacy of figure of speech. For then, in even the strongest of demonstrations, there would always be the fallacy of figure of speech. But, generally, when a demonstration goes from a term standing merely confusedly to one standing determinately, enthymematically at any rate, it is [an instance of] the fallacy of figure of speech, [especially] if no variation at all is made with respect to another term and its dispositions; although, at the same time, there may be a fallacy of [affirming] the consequent, just as in the proposed example. If, however, it were argued that "every man is an animal; therefore, an animal is a man," [then] even though in the antecedent it[33] supposits merely confusedly and in the consequent determinately; nevertheless, because the sign[34] added to man in the antecedent is not added to it in the consequent, it is not an instance of the fallacy of figure of speech.

According to this mode, all such sophisms as the following are in error: "for every part of a continuum there is some smaller part; therefore, some part is smaller than every part of a continuum." The antecedent is true, because any singular [instance of it] is true, and the consequent is false because any singular [instance of it] is false. But the consequent is not valid, because "part" in the antecedent supposits merely confusedly and in the consequent it supposits determinately. But because the fallacy of [affirming the] consequent is more evident in such propositions than the fallacy of figure of speech, therefore, when the fallacy in the consequent is discussed, different examples will be adduced.

Similarly, arguing from a term standing determinately or merely confusedly to the same term standing confusedly and distributively[35] is [an instance of] the fal-

---

[33]it: *animal*, because it is the only term in the antecedent that supposits merely confusedly; it supposits merely confusedly because it mediately follows a term (*man*) in the subject that has a universal affirmative sign ("every"). See Chapter 73, "On Merely Confused Supposition," in book I of *Summa Logicae*.

[34]sign: i.e., "every," otherwise known as the universal affirmative specifically, and a syncategorematic term or quantifier generally.

[35]merely confusedly: "Ockham divides terms with confused supposition into 'merely confused' and 'confused and distributive.'

lacy of figure of speech, although it is also a fallacy of [affirming the] consequent here, just as in this: "you doubt something to be true; therefore, you do not know something to be true." Hence, if one were to argue "that which you doubt, you do not know; you doubt something to be true; therefore, you do not know something to be true" is [an instance of] the fallacy of figure of speech, because in the antecedent the word "true" stands determinately, but in the consequent it stands merely confusedly.

Similarly, this: "that which is not something, differs from this; Socrates is not every man; therefore, Socrates differs from every man," for in the antecedent the word "man" stands determinately on account of the preceding negation, whereas in the consequent it stands confusedly and distributively.

It is necessary to know, however, that the fallacy of figure of speech happens to occur not only from a different mode of suppositing the same term, but also from a different mode of suppositing different terms, provided that the corresponding other term is not changed. Hence, the following is [an instance of] the fallacy of figure of speech: "every man is an animal; therefore, substance is every man," and the same holds for similar [propositions].

Moreover, not only does the third mode [of this fallacy] arise from a different mode of signification, – which frequently results from the mode of signifying a categorematic and a syncategorematic term, – but it also arises from different modes of signifying incom-

---

See King, in "Supposition," *William of Ockham: Summa Logicae.*

plex [terms] in different categories.[36] So when, because it is believed that an argument will be valid if it is argued from all the terms of the same category, because similarly arguing from the terms of different categories is [considered] an acceptable argument, – even though it is not, – then the fallacy of the figure of speech occurs. For it is believed, on account of the similarity of expressions, that it is just as likely for someone to argue from these terms as from those, and therefore a deception will occur because of the fallacy of figure of speech.

However, it should first be understood that the fallacy of figure of speech does not always arise when arguing from terms of different categories because, generally, when the premises are purely assertoric and in the present [tense], categorical and direct, and arranged in mood and in figure,[37] it is not the fallacy of figure of speech that arises, whatever the terms may be. And it is all one whether all the terms be of the same category or different. Hence, the syllogism "every man is an animal; a white thing is a man; therefore, a white thing is an animal" is just as valid as this one: "every man is an animal; Socrates is a man; therefore, Socrates is an animal." And so it is, in general, in similar cases.

And therefore, in order to attribute the fallacy of fig-

---

[36]categories: there are ten in all, as described by Aristotle in "Categories" in *Organon*.

[37]mood and figure: see "Categorical Syllogisms: Major, Middle and Minor Terms" in Spade, Paul Vincent. *Thoughts, Words and Things: An Introduction to Late Mediaeval Logic and Semantic Theory*. Version 1.2: December 27, 2007

ure of speech [to a proposition], it is not sufficient to say that one category is commuted into another; a more specific reason is needed. It should be understood, therefore, that although arguing syllogistically entails arguing as much from the terms of different categories as from those of the same category, arguing non-syllogistically often entails arguing from terms of the same category and not from those of different ones. And this can happen in many ways; for example, it can happen on account of the different distributive signs.

To clarify, it should be understood that just as different interrogative signs correspond to different categories, to the effect that a response to different interrogatives is made through the incomplex [expressions] of different categories, – for example, if someone asked what a man is, a fitting response is that he is an animal; and if someone asked what sort of man he is, a fitting response is that he is white or musical, but not that he is an animal; and if someone asked where a man is, a fitting response is that he is in the marketplace or in the fields, and so on and so forth, – so too, different distributive signs correspond to different categories, just as "anyone," "anything," and the like, correspond to the category of substance. But it should be understood that such distributive [sign]s are equally applicable to all purely absolute nouns, whether these nouns signify substances or qualities or other kinds of things. To the category of quantity, however, correspond the distributives "however much" and "however many," in the place of which "how much" and "how many" are sometimes used instead. To the category of quality corresponds the [distributive] sign "of whatever sort." To the category "where," the sign "wherever." And to the category "when," the sign "whenever," and so on, unless nouns greatly fail us.

The distributive [sign corresponding to] substance, or the distributive [sign] corresponding to purely absolute nouns, differs from other [signs], however, because it sometimes happens as well that connotative or relative nouns are assumed as purely absolute nouns. Hence, the following mode of arguing is equally valid: "whatever is a man, is an animal; bicubit is a man; therefore, bicubit is an animal" just as this one is: "whatever is a man, is an animal; Socrates is a man; therefore, Socrates is an animal," and this is because the major [premise] is equivalent to "every man is an animal." But this is not the case with other distributive [signs], because under other distributive [signs] it never occurs – while maintaining the proper mode of reasoning – to subsume anything except an incomplex [expression] consistent with and appropriate to such a distributive [sign]. For which reason, arguing from such [reasoning], it is necessary to know the natures of the categories; namely, what they signify, which things they signify, how they signify, and that not all categories signify one thing, but rather many of them signify more than one thing, although not all univocally nor with the same mode of signification. And whoever knows this is close to seeing the truth in many things, according to the Philosopher in his his book *On Sophistical Refutations*.

It should be known, therefore, that whenever a major premise having the distributive sign "however great" or "however many" is taken, if any incomplex [expression] is subsumed under it except for what happens to answer the question "how much" or "how many," it is [an instance of] the fallacy of figure of speech on account of the distinction of categories. And this [is] because, if some incomplex [expression] that properly responded to such a question were subsumed under it, there would be no fallacy. And, therefore, if anyone believes that, on this account, it is possible to subsume one term for another in the minor [premise], as happens in many other [cases], he will be deceived by the fallacy of figure of speech; just as "how much A is, that much B is; A is wood; therefore, B is wood." And yet, if instead of this term "wood" the term "tricubit" were used, it would be a valid argument, thus arguing "how much A is, that much B is; A is a tricubit; therefore, B is a tricubit."

Similarly, if after the sign "of whatever sort" in the major premise, some incomplex [expression] is accepted under it in the minor premise, which does not answer the question posed by "of what sort," there is the fallacy of figure of speech. And if an incomplex [expression] is accepted that properly answers the question posed by "of what sort," the argument will be valid. Just as the following is [an instance of] the fallacy of figure of speech: "[a thing] of whatever sort runs, disputes; Socrates runs; therefore, Socrates disputes," but not this one: "[a thing] of whatever sort runs, disputes; a black one runs; therefore, a black one disputes."

Similarly, the following is [an example of] the fallacy of figure of speech: "whenever there is an accident, then there is its subject; an accident is inherent; therefore, a subject is inherent," but not this: "whenever there is an accident, there is its subject; the accident exists at this time; therefore, the subject exists at this time."

Similarly this is [an example of] the fallacy of figure of speech: "wherever there is substance, there is quantity; an angel is substance; therefore, an angel is quantity," but not this: "wherever there is substance, there is quantity; substance exists in this place; therefore, quantity exists in this place." And so it is possible to argue in other [cases] where a distributive sign corresponds to an interrogative one, to which a suitable answer may be given by means of the incomplex [expressions] of some category, but not others.

However, there is a special difficulty regarding distributive [signs] of substance. For which [reason], it must be known that when a distributive [sign] of substance is used in a proposition purely in the present [tense] and purely assertoric, it does not matter what is accepted under the minor premise. And therefore the following mode of argumentation is valid: "whatever you buy, you consume; you buy raw meat; therefore you consume raw meat," "whatever is a corporeal substance is a quantity; the body of Christ is a corporeal substance; therefore, the body of Christ is a quantity," and so forth. But, in such a way that no determination of composition is accepted in the minor [premise] that was not accepted in the major [premise] while, simultaneously, one number[38] is not

---

[38]number: a (logical) quantity or quantifier; e.g., singular, particular, indefinite, or universal. For instance, "every" is a universal quantifier, and "some" is an indefinite quantifier.

commuted into another, because if either of these things should occur, then it is [an instance of] the fallacy of figure of speech, as will be shown. Hence, in many ways, when premises arranged in mood and in figure are not accepted, nor their equivalents, the fallacy of figure of speech occurs: or [it occurs] by employing a noun other than the one given in answer to the question "what is it" about some one thing; for sometimes this happens when arguing from propositions in the present [tense], or from propositions in the past or future [tenses], or from propositions in [a particular] modality.

If it is argued from propositions in the present [tense] and that are assertoric, this can occur; or [it can occur] by adding some determination[39] through which it acts as a response, partially at least, to the question put by another interrogative about some one thing, other than "what is it." For example, if it is argued that "whatever runs is a body; a man runs quickly; therefore, a man is a body [that runs] quickly," because "quickly" is added to the minor premise, such that it responds to a question other than "what is it," then this is [an instance of] the fallacy of figure of speech. And yet, if the determination "actually" were used, it would be a valid argument, thus arguing "whatever runs is a body; a man actually runs; therefore, man actually is a body." Hence, in general, in such a mode of argumentation, when some determination is added to the minor premise which may or may not agree with it, it causes the fallacy of figure of speech, whereas another [determination] does not cause the fallacy of figure of speech. However, such a

---

[39]determination: qualifier, or qualification.

[determinative] sign could be accepted in the minor premise such that there would not be a fallacy of figure of speech. Just as it might be said that "how" is an interrogative adverb to which it is proper to respond with such words as "quickly," "rapidly," "slowly," "violently," and so forth, and that the sign "howsoever" corresponds to it; with that said, the following mode of argumentation will be valid: "howsoever something runs, it is a body; a man runs rapidly; therefore, a man is a body [that runs] rapidly."

Similarly, the following is [an instance of] the fallacy of figure of speech: "every material substance has one part distant from another; the body of Christ in the sacrament of the Altar is a material substance; therefore, the body of Christ in the sacrament of the Altar has one part distant from another."

Similarly this: "every body is a quantum; the body of Christ is a body in the sacrament of the Altar; therefore, the body of Christ is a quantum in the sacrament of the Altar."

Similarly this: "every body is circumscribed in place; the body of Christ is a body in the sacrament of the Altar; therefore, the body of Christ is circumscribed in place in the sacrament of the Altar."

Similarly this, according to one opinion: "every material substance is a quantum; the body of Christ is a material substance in the sacrament of the Altar; therefore, the body of Christ is a quantity in the sacrament of the Altar."

Similarly this: "whatever is a substance is a quantity; the body of Christ is a substance in the sacrament of the Altar; therefore, the body of Christ is a quantity in the sacrament of the Altar." And yet, arguing like this: "wheresoever something is a substance, it is [also] a quantity; the body of Christ is a substance in the sacrament of the Altar; therefore, the body of Christ is a quantity in the sacrament of the Altar" is a valid argument.

And thus it is clear that, by substituting the sign "wheresoever" for the sign "whatsoever," no fallacy results [when] taking something as a response to the question "where." For this reason, it is extremely necessary to understand what sorts of category they are, and what and how they mean, so that it may be known from the many cases [in which they appear] whether there is the fallacy of figure of speech. From the foregoing it is clear that the following is not a fallacy: "wheresoever something has quantity inherent in itself, there is a quantum; the substance of the body of Christ has quantity inherent in itself in the sacrament of the Altar; therefore, the substance of the body of Christ is a quantity in the sacrament of the Altar." Nor this: "wheresoever something has length, width, and depth inherent in itself, it is long, wide, and deep there; but the substance of the body of Christ has length, width, and depth inherent in itself in the sacrament of the Altar; therefore, the substance of the body of Christ is long, wide, and deep in the sacrament of the Altar." Nor this: "wheresoever some substance has extension inherent in itself, it is extended there; the substance of the body of Christ has extension inherent in itself in the sacrament of the Altar; therefore, the substance of the body of Christ is extended in the sacrament of the Altar."

Otherwise, it is possible to err through the fallacy of figure of speech by arguing in such a manner, by changing one number into another, for instance, [by changing] a singular into a plural, thus: "whatever is known, is known through discovery or instruction; these things are known – by showing one thing known through discovery and another through instruction; therefore, these things are known through discovery or instruction."

Similarly, this: "every divine person is God; the Father and the Son are divine persons; therefore, the Father and the Son are gods."

Similarly, this: "every divine person producing a person is a first principle of the Holy Spirit; the Father and the Son are divine persons producing a person; therefore, the Father and the Son are first principles of the Holy Spirit."

It must be known, however, that such a mode of reasoning can scarcely or never be impeded by two such propositions except when the argument is disjunctive and when a significant term is understood as some one thing which is multiple persons, as it is with God, who is one God but multiple persons. Similarly, one principle of the Holy Spirit is two persons. However, arguing enthymematically and changing a singular number into a plural is often a fallacy of figure of speech in other cases. And this occurs wherever the term does not signify many; just as in the following: "the sun is a body; therefore, suns are bodies"; and in the following: "a phoenix is an animal; therefore, phoenixes are animals," and this is because of a false implication in the consequence. And, therefore, it is

the only consequence as [with] this: "a man is an animal; therefore, men are animals." And such false consequences can be reduced to the first mode, in which
a deception arises on account of the diverse grammatical accidents of diverse expressions.

Otherwise, such a mode of argumentation errs with
respect to the fallacy of figure of speech, by arguing
from propositions in the past or future [tense], and in
this case by arguing either from all [propositions] in
the past, or from one in the past and one in the
present. And in the same way, in like proportion,
something must be said about those [propositions] in
the future [tense]. If in the first case, what is assumed
in the minor [premise] is posited either of the subject
or of the predicate; the propositions must be resolved
into equivalent propositions that can be arranged in
mood and in figure; and then the strategy that has
been given must be employed for how to syllogize
from propositions in the past and future. For example,
if it is argued that "whatever you bought yesterday,
you ate today; you bought raw meat yesterday; therefore, you ate raw meat today," the major premise
must be resolved into its equivalent: "everything
bought yesterday was eaten by you today"; the minor
into its equivalent: "the raw meat was bought by you
yesterday"; and the conclusion into its equivalent:
"the raw meat was eaten by you today." And if the
subject in each of these [propositions] is taken for the
things that were, the syllogism holds. But if the subject of the conclusion is taken [to stand] for the things
that are, it does not hold, and it is more [on account
of] the fallacy of accident than that of figure of
speech. But if what is assumed is posited on the part

of the predicate, [then] it is always the fallacy of figure of speech. Hence, the following is [an instance of] the fallacy of figure of speech: "whatever you bought yesterday, you ate today; yesterday you bought raw meat; therefore, you ate raw meat today." And the fallacy of figure of speech will be all the clearer if the major premise was in the present [tense] and the minor [premise was] in the past or future. For this reason, the following is [an instance of] the fallacy of figure of speech, according to the opinion that holds quantity to be no different from substance and quality: "whatever was yesterday, is today; Socrates was of a bicubital quantity yesterday; therefore, Socrates is of a bicubital quantity today." Similarly, this: "whatever was, still is; Socrates was of a triangular shape; therefore Socrates is of a triangular shape." Likewise: "whatever was, is; fire brought light and warmed; therefore, fire brings light and warms." For in all such propositions there is the fallacy of figure of speech.

And yet, when taking [the terms as] purely absolute nouns, there is no fallacy. Just as this is a valid argument: "whatever was, is; a man was; therefore a man is." And similarly this: "whatever was, is; whiteness was; therefore whiteness is." And similarly this: "whatever was, is; Socrates was a man; therefore Socrates is a man." And similarly this: "whatever was, is; this whiteness was a color; therefore, this whiteness is a color." And yet, according to the opinion that posits that quantity is nothing other than substance and quality, this is a fallacy of figure of speech: "whatever was, still is; this substance was a quantity; therefore, this substance still is a quantity."

But this is a valid argument: "whenever anything was a substance, then it was a quantity; this substance was a substance; therefore, this substance was a quantity." Similarly, this is a fallacy of figure of speech: whatever is, previously was; A is like B; therefore, A previously was like B." Similarly, this is the fallacy of figure of speech: "whatever was, still is; this body was conjoined to that body; therefore this body is still conjoined to that body." And yet, this is a valid argument: "whatever was, is; whiteness was; therefore whiteness is." And just as has been said about propositions in the past, so, in like proportion, it must be said about propositions in the future.

Otherwise, the fallacy of figure of speech arises from the difference in categories in modal propositions, for example, by arguing: "whatever God can do by means of a secondary cause, he can do by himself; but God can do a meritorious act by means of a secondary cause; therefore, he can do a meritorious act by himself." Response: this last argument is [an instance of] the fallacy of figure of speech, because if the term was taken as purely absolute, it would be a valid argument; for example, this is a valid argument: "whatever God can do by means of a secondary cause, he can do by himself; but God can make fire by means of a secondary cause; therefore, etc." And therefore, if on account of the similarity of expressions someone believes that one argument is just as valid as another, he will be deceived by the fallacy of figure of speech.

Nevertheless, it should be known that if "a meritorious act" were put in the place of the subject, it would not be the fallacy of figure of speech. Hence, this is not [an instance of] the fallacy of figure of speech: "whatever God can do by means of a secondary cause, etc.; but every meritorious act God can do by means of a secondary cause; therefore, every meritorious act God can do by himself," because the conclusion is true if the premises are true, whether the subject is taken for things that exist or not.

Similarly, this is the fallacy of figure of speech: "everything God can make without another, totally distinct thing; a white thing is something distinct from whiteness; therefore, God can make a white thing without whiteness." And yet, this conclusion easily follows: "a white thing God can make without whiteness," because that thing which is white God can make without whiteness; and yet, this is impossible: "a white thing God makes without whiteness."

Similarly, this is [an instance of] the fallacy of figure of speech: "God can cause every possible thing that is not God; the truth of this proposition 'God causes nothing' can exist; therefore, God can cause the truth of this proposition," for this expression "the truth of this proposition" is not an incomplex, purely absolute one.

It is necessary to know, however, that this mode of the fallacy of figure of speech occurs not only in such discourses composed of many premises, but also in consequences and enthymemes; because this mode occurs not only when one category is commuted into another, but also when a distributive sign corresponding to one category is initially found in the major premise, but later appears under the incomplex [term] of another category. Because the Philosopher never says that the [fallacy of] figure of speech is from the commutation of one category into another, but that because the categories are different and signify the same things in different ways, the consequents [resulting] from the incomplex [terms] of some categories are, therefore, often invalid. And yet, if, instead of those, the incomplex [terms] of another category were posited, the consequences would be valid; just as this is a valid consequence: "a man was an animal; therefore, an animal was a man." Similarly, "whiteness was blackness; therefore, blackness was whiteness." Similarly, "whiteness can be a color; therefore, a color can be whiteness." Similarly, consequences such as these are valid: "whiteness ceases being whiteness; therefore, whiteness ceases being"; "a man stops being a man; therefore, a man stops being," and so forth. Which, therefore, are valid consequences because the terms from which they are composed do not signify something directly or indirectly, nor do they signify something primarily and principally and something secondarily, nor do they signify something affirmatively or something negatively, but they signify all their significata in the same way. Which, according to Aristotle's principles, is not true except with respect to incomplex [terms] in the genus of substance, and to abstract [terms] in the genus of quality, to which concrete supposita correspond for things [that are] distinct from those for which the abstract [terms] supposit, and therefore the consequences from such terms are valid and others are not. For this reason, if anyone believes that consimilar consequences are just as valid for some terms as they are for others, he will be deceived by the fallacy of figure of speech.

Hence, the following is [an instance of] the fallacy of figure of speech with respect to this mode: "white will cease being white tomorrow; therefore, white will cease being tomorrow"; "motion will cease being motion when it stops moving; therefore, motion will cease being when it stops moving," just as the following is [an instance of] the fallacy of figure of speech: "a form divisibly acquired will cease being divisibly acquired when it stops moving; therefore, a form divisibly acquired will cease being when it stops moving." Similarly, this: "a meritorious act God can do, without an efficient will; therefore, God can do a meritorious act without an efficient will." Similarly, this: "this truth God can make – by demonstrating the truth of this: God makes nothing; – therefore, God can make this truth." Similarly, this: "man from eternity was God; therefore, God from eternity was man."

And for this example and for the others before it, it must be understood that although this noun "man" according to the usage of philosophers is a purely absolute term, signifying one significatum no more directly than another; nevertheless, according to the usage of theologians, it is not so purely absolute, for if it were, it would be convertible with the noun "humanity." And so, just as this must be denied: "The Son of God is humanity," this too would need to be denied: "The Son of God is man," because it is false. And therefore, according to the usage of theologians, this noun "man" connotes or consignifies, at least potentially, a divine suppositum, which although he was not man, he could, however, have been man. And because of this, when I offered many examples of the noun "man," I spoke according to the usage of philosophers.

Similarly, this is the fallacy of figure of speech: "The Son of God cannot be man; therefore, man cannot be the Son of God," for the same reason.

However, to understand why it is the fallacy of figure of speech in the preceding proposition is not a matter for the logician, but for whoever knows not only logic perfectly but other arts or special sciences, and therefore whoever in every argument knows how to assign the fallacy of figure of speech is close to seeing the truth in every science.

It should also be understood that although such consequences have a general defect, nevertheless, sometimes some of them, by virtue of the matter, can hold. And then, in order to show that some of these consequences hold by virtue of the matter and others do not, it is necessary to recur to the second principal mode of this fallacy and to the art confided therein. Nor is it inappropriate that the two modes of the same fallacy should sometimes concur in the same argument.

Furthermore, all paralogisms – those, that is, in which the argument proceeds from premises possessing some determinateness to a conclusion lacking that determinateness – must be reduced to this [first] mode, although a few such paralogisms can be reduced to the second principal mode. Hence, this is [an instance of] the fallacy of figure of speech: "you do not have a denarius sadly; and [yet] you give a denarius sadly; therefore, you give what you do not have."

Similarly, this: "you do not have one single denarius; and [yet] you give one single denarius; therefore, you give what you do not have." And the reason for the fallacy of figure of speech in such [cases] is this: because if, in such premises, instead of these terms: "a denarius sadly" and "one single denarius," purely absolute terms were used [instead], there would not be any fallacy with respect to the same conclusion. Just as this is not a fallacy: "you do not have a rational animal; you give a rational animal; therefore, you give what you do not have"; nor this: "you give an ox and do not have an ox; therefore, you give what you do not have."

But is this possibly [an instance of] the fallacy of figure of speech: "you give a white ox; and you do not have a white ox; therefore, you give what you do not have"? It must be said that this is a valid argument, because the lack of determinateness in the conclusion does not always constitute a fallacy of figure of speech; but when that determinateness is [found] in one category, then it does; but when [it is found] in another, it does not. Hence, this clearly follows: "you give one denarius; and you do not have one denarius; therefore, you give what you do not have"; however, this does not follow: "you give an ox in this place; and you do not have an ox in this place; therefore you give what you do not have." Nor can a general rule be given [as to] when such a consequence is valid and when it is not.

Similarly, the fallacy of figure of speech can occur

when some terms signify something negatively and
something affirmatively, just as in this example: "you
give one single denarius; and you do not have one
single denarius; therefore, you give what you do not
have." Hence, because this "one single" signifies sev-
eral things negatively; as a result such a consequence
is invalid.

Not only, however, does the fallacy of figure of
speech occur because categorematic and syncategorematic incomplex [terms] signify differently, or because different categories signify differently, or because some terms signify something negatively,
something positively, and something negatively and
positively; but also because some terms are common
to many, and some are discrete,[40] among which
should be included proper nouns and demonstrative
and relative pronouns.

And it is the mode [that occurs] when some argument
would hold if, instead of a common term or instead of
a term including a common term as part of it, a proper
noun, demonstrative pronoun, or relative pronoun
were posited; but because another term is posited than
a demonstrative or relative pronoun or a proper noun,
or vice versa, the argument is invalid. For example, if
it is argued that "Marcus can be different from Tullius; Marcus is Tullius; therefore Marcus can be different from himself," this is a valid argument if "Marcus" is the proper noun of this man and he is the same
[person] as "Tullius." If, however, instead of this
[proper] noun "Tullius," a common noun like "musi-

---

[40]discrete: See item 70, "On the Division of Personal Supposition"
in Book I of the *Summa Logicae*.

cian" were posited, or if the same common noun were added to it, the argument would be invalid; for example, it does not follow that "Marcus can be different from a musician, or from Tullius the musician; Marcus is a musician, or Tullius is a musician; therefore, Marcus can be different from himself."

Similarly, this is a valid argument: "Marcus is third from Socrates and from Tullius; therefore, Marcus is third from himself"; but this argument is invalid: "Marcus is third from Socrates and from a man; therefore, Marcus is third from himself." And yet, there is no difference except in the one [case where] a common noun is used and in the other where, instead of a common noun, a proper noun is used. For this reason, if someone believes that this argument is valid when a common noun is used, just as that one is valid when a proper noun is used, he is deceived by the fallacy of figure of speech, as long as he believes, on account of the similarity, [that] the one term is just as valid as the other.

Similarly, this is a valid argument: "Marcus is not third from himself and from Socrates; Marcus is Tullius; therefore, Marcus is not third from Socrates and from Tullius." And, nevertheless, if instead of this proper noun "Tullius," the common noun "man" were used, the argument would be invalid, because it does not follow that "Marcus is not third from himself and from Socrates; Marcus is a man; therefore, Marcus is not third from Socrates and from a man." And thus it is clear that sometimes, when a proper noun is used, the argument is valid, and when a common noun is used, it is not. And this is one [sub]mode of the third principal mode.

Nevertheless, it must not be said that it is always the fallacy of figure of speech when a proper noun is taken instead of a common noun, or vice versa. Hence, they err who say that this is the fallacy of figure of speech: "Coriscus is different from Coriscus the musician; Coriscus is Coriscus the musician; therefore, Coriscus is different from himself," if Coriscus is a proper noun and not equivocal; for if it were an equivocal noun, it would be [an instance of] the fallacy of figure of speech. That it is not, however, [an instance of] the fallacy of figure of speech, is obvious; for it follows [that] "Coriscus is different from Coriscus the musician; therefore, Coriscus is not Coriscus the musician," and it follows [that] "Coriscus is not Coriscus the musician; therefore, Coriscus the musician is not Coriscus." Similarly, it follows that "Coriscus is Coriscus the musician; therefore, Coriscus the musician is Coriscus." From these two [statements], the main conclusion follows, which is this: "Coriscus the musician is not Coriscus; Coriscus the musician is Coriscus; therefore, Coriscus is not Coriscus"; and, further, this: "therefore, Coriscus is different from himself."

Nor is it valid to say that it does not follow that "Coriscus is different from Coriscus the musician; therefore, Coriscus is not Coriscus the musician" because this does follow: "Coriscus is different from Coriscus the musician; therefore, Coriscus the musician is different from Coriscus" and, further, that "therefore, Coriscus is different from Coriscus"; and finally that "therefore, Coriscus is not Coriscus the musician"; therefore, from beginning to end, [this is an instance of the fallacy of figure of speech].

It must be said, therefore, that such reasoning is valid from purely assertoric propositions and those purely in the present [tense]. But this reasoning is not valid: "Coriscus can be different from Coriscus the musician; Coriscus is Coriscus the musician; therefore, Coriscus can be different from himself"; and yet, if instead of the term "Coriscus the musician" some demonstrative or relative pronoun were posited, or some proper noun, the reasoning would be valid.

And if the cause of this were sought, it must be said that the cause is that multiple affirmative [proposition]s, – in which common terms or pronouns, or proper nouns with common terms, are used, – can have more causes of truth than if a proper noun or pronoun were used in their place. For the statement "Coriscus can be different from Coriscus the musician" can have all of the following causes of truth: "Coriscus can be different from Coriscus"; "Coriscus can be different from the musician"; "Coriscus is able not to be Coriscus the musician." And not all these causes of truth can include "Coriscus can be different from himself" or "Coriscus can be different from Coriscus."

And if it be said, then, that this is [an instance of] the fallacy of [affirming the] consequent, it must be replied that it is not inappropriate for the fallacy of [affirming the] consequent to occur here. If, however, someone should be deceived because he sees that such a mode of arguing holds in consimilar expressions, he will be deceived by the fallacy of figure of speech.

With respect to this mode, such sophisms err: "whenever some things are really the same, wherever one of
them is, the rest of them are; but the substance of the
body of Christ, and the substance of the body of
Christ having one part distant from another, are really
the same thing, and the body of Christ is, in the sacrament of the Alter, the substance of the body of Christ;
therefore, the body of Christ is, in the sacrament of
the Altar, having one part distant from another," because if instead of the expression "substance of the
body of Christ having one part distant from another"
a proper noun, or a pronoun, were used, indicating
that thing which is the substance of the body of Christ
having one part distant from another, it would be a
valid argument.

Similarly, this is [an instance of] the fallacy of figure
of speech: "this substance is a substance having one
part distant from another; this thing is a substance in
the sacrament of the Altar; therefore, this thing is a
substance having one part distant from another in the
sacrament of the Altar." And yet, if in the conclusion,
instead of the expression "a substance having one part
distant from another" a proper noun or demonstrative
pronoun were used, it would be a valid argument.
And for this reason, it is [an instance of] the fallacy of
figure of speech with respect to the the other previ-
ously-stated mode.

Similarly, this is [an instance of] the fallacy of figure
of speech: "when some things are actually the same,
one thing cannot exist without the other; but Socrates
and a similar [person] are actually the same; there-

fore, Socrates cannot exist unless he is similar," because if, instead of this term "similar," a proper noun suppositing for the similar [person] were used, or a pronoun indicating the same similar [person], the argument would be valid.

Similarly, [an instance of] the fallacy of figure of speech exists in such [cases]: "a mobile thing, when it exists, is able not to be moved; therefore, motion is really distinct from a mobile thing." Similarly, this: "this existing substance itself is able not to be quantified; therefore, substance is really distinct from quantity." Similarly, according to Aristotle's principles, "substance, although it does not cease to exist, is able not to be quantity; therefore, substance is not really the same as quantity" and "whiteness, although it does not cease to exist, is able not to be similarity; therefore, whiteness is not the same thing as similarity." And yet, in all these [cases], if instead of the common term a proper noun or a demonstrative pronoun were used, the argument would be valid.

It should be known, however, that although the aforesaid consequents do not hold when placing the common terms in the predicate of a categorical proposition, if they were placed on the part of the subject in a copulative [proposition], the consequents would be valid. For example, it follows that "a mobile thing can exist in A; and then motion is able not to exist, although the mobile thing exists then; therefore, motion is not actually the same thing as a mobile thing." Similarly, it follows that "a substance can exist at some time; and then a quantum is able not to exist, although a substance then exists; therefore, a quantum is not really the same as a substance." But the second of the premises then will be false.

And the reason that one mode of arguing holds and the other does not is that "quantum" can be a substance [even] when the substance itself will not be quantified, just as "white" will be Socrates [even] when Socrates [himself] will not be white. Suppose that Socrates is white now and that he will be black tomorrow: the following is true then: "white will be Socrates tomorrow"; and this is false: "Socrates will be white tomorrow." And this is because one mode of arguing holds and the other does not.

And whence does this cause arise? It must be said that it arises from the fact that the other mode of signifying has the noun "Socrates" and the term "white," because "white" signifies Socrates in the nominative case when Socrates is white, and it signifies whiteness in the oblique case, which can be eliminated while Socrates remains. Similarly this, which may be true according to one opinion: "quantity can be substance [even] when substance will not be quantity," the reason being, according to them, is that this term "quantity" signifies that one part of a thing is distant from another, and God can make it so that the substance remains even though one part is not distant from another.[41] And thus is it with all consimilar [cases] in which a different mode of signifying causes the fallacy of figure of speech in such sophisms. On this account, in order to recognize the third principal mode of [the fallacy of] figure of speech, it is neces-

---

[41]in other words, the substance remains without quantity. A solid understanding of transubstantiation, and sacramental theology of the Eucharist, may help in this discussion.

sary to know what things the terms signify and how they signify them; namely, whether in the nominative or in the oblique case, affirmatively or negatively, whether as categorematic or syncategorematic terms, and whether as proper or common nouns, although this last [case] can be reduced to the second principal mode.

Hence, whatever may be said about a distinction among these modes, it must be nevertheless be maintained, according to Aristotle's doctrine, that there is always [an instance of] the fallacy of figure of speech when it is not possible to argue similarly from different terms because of a diversity of expressions that seem similar, on account of which similarity some [people] may conclude that they must be argued about similarly.

It must always be observed, however, that – whenever premises are arranged in mood and in figure, according to the rules given at the beginning of this treatise on syllogisms, both uniform and mixed – there is never [an instance of] the fallacy of figure of speech.

Chapter 11. On the Fallacy of Accident

After the fallacies in diction, something must be said about the fallacies outside of diction, the first of which is the fallacy of accident.

About this fallacy, it should be known that "accident" is not taken here in the [same] sense as earlier, where an accident was counted as one of the five universals, but rather "accident" is taken here for any term that can be a subject or predicate distinct from another. Hence, any term that can be subject or predicate of a proposition can be, and is, an accident with respect to something, because it is a predicable or subjectible term discrete from another predicable.

The cause of the appearance of this fallacy is the identity of the predication of one term with another, that is, the reason it deceives is because we see a term to be predicated of another [term] affirmatively or negatively, and we believe that whatever is said about the one is said about the other.

The cause of [its] non-existence is that, although one term is predicated of another, it does not follow that whatever is said about the accident, that is, about one of them, must be said, on this account, about the other; nor is it necessary that what is said about the one is said about the other in the same way.

And, therefore, the general response to all paralogisms of accident is to say that it is not necessary that the conclusion should follow from the premises, that is, that it is not necessary that what is said about the predicate of the conclusion be said about the subject of the conclusion on account of their union with one another in the premises. Just as the extremes "man... ass" need not be conjoined by predication, by saying, for example, [that] "a man is an ass," even though these two terms "man" and "ass" may be conjoined by predication with the middle term "animal," by say- ing, for example, [that] "an ass is an animal," "a man is an animal." And this is the general response to all paralogisms of accident.

But beyond this general response, it is necessary, ac- cording to Aristotle, to explain "how so"; that is, it is necessary to assign some specific, evident rule [as to] why it does not follow, and for the different [cases] it is necessary to assign different, specific rules.

To be clear, it should be known that there are two principal modes of this fallacy. One mode is when certain things that are joined by predication with a third [thing] in the premises end up joined together in the conclusion. The second mode is when certain things joined by different propositions with a certain thing end up, by a single proposition, joined with the same third [thing].

And it must be known that the fallacy of accident is not to be ascribed to a variation of the middle term, because the middle term need not vary in the fallacy of accident. Here is an example of a middle term that does not vary at all: "Socrates is a man; Plato is a man; therefore, Plato is Socrates." But the fallacy of accident always, or frequently, occurs as a result of the identity of the middle; for when, because some things are conjoined by predication in an unvaried middle term, it is believed that they should be conjoined together by predication, but it is not necessary, – it is the fallacy of accident. But no sufficient general rule can be given here, because it is neither by variation of the middle term, as has been said, nor by reduplication[42] of the minor proposition over the major extreme, because frequently such reduplication is impossible, and yet the syllogism is valid. For example, this is a valid syllogism: "every man is a stone; every whiteness is a man; therefore, every whiteness is a stone," and yet the following reduplication is impossible: "every whiteness is a man insofar as it is a stone." A general rule, therefore, cannot be given for every paralogism by which the fallacy of accident might be sufficiently recognized in every case.

It must be known, therefore, that the first mode of the fallacy of accident is when the premises are arranged in figure but not in mood. And this can happen either when the premises are simply categorical, in the present [tense], and assertoric, or when they are modal, or [when] one [premise] is modal and the other [is] assertoric, or [when] they are in the past or future [tense].

Hence, according to this type of the fallacy of accident all useless combinations, whether uniform or mixed, are in error, which the Philosopher discusses in his *Prior [Analytics]*, and which was discussed earlier. And, therefore, [in order] to know when this type

---

[42]reduplication: the qualification of a term in order to disambiguate its meaning.

of the fallacy of accident occurs, one must know all those rules, and one must know with respect to which of those rules the paralogism errs, and therefore one must know how to assign different rules to different cases.

Hence, this is [an instance of] the fallacy of accident: "[someone] coming is known by you; Coriscus is coming; therefore, Coriscus is known by you." And, in assigning [a cause], you ought to mention "how so," and to say that this is the fallacy of accident, because the major [premise] is particular or indefinite in an affirmative syllogism of the first figure; which would not be a fallacy if the major were in a universal proposition. Hence, the following is not a fallacy: "every[one] coming is known by you; Coriscus is coming; therefore, Coriscus is known by you," because the major [premise] is universal.

Similarly, the following is [an instance of] the fallacy of accident: "every man is an animal; every ass is an animal; therefore, every ass is a man." And the general assignment [of cause] ought to be this, that this is the fallacy of accident, because although "animal" is predicated of man, it does not follow that whenever "animal" is said of something, "man" is also said of it, in such a way that animal is said of man. And when mentioning "how so," you ought specifically to say that this is the fallacy of accident, because the argument proceeds from all affirmatives in the second figure. And so, for different [cases], different rules ought to be assigned, and without those rules it generally cannot be known when the fallacy of accident occurs and when it does not.

When, therefore, the fallacy of accident occurs with respect to this mode of arguing from propositions [that are] purely categorical, purely assertoric, and purely in the present [tense], it is easy to recognize according to Aristotle's rules, as communicated in his *Prior Analytics*, concerning the uniform generation of assertoric syllogisms, except in one case, namely, divine matters, where it must be conceded that one simple thing is multiple persons, who are actually distinct from one another, as was touched on earlier, because the fallacy of accident often occurs in such terms and not in others. Hence, this is the fallacy of accident: "every divine essence is the Father; the Son is the divine essence; therefore, the Son is the Father." And a specific rule must be assigned [to such arguments] as follows: because one essence comprises multiple persons, who are distinct amongst each other, it does not follow that every name of a person of whom the name of the essence is predicated is predicated of the name of another person.

Similarly, this is [an instance of] the fallacy of accident: "this essence is the Father; this essence is the Son; therefore, the Son is the Father." And a consimilar rule applies to it; for one essence is multiple persons, therefore it does not follow that, although the names of those persons are predicated of the proper name of that essence or of the pronoun indicating that essence, on this account the one name of one person is predicated of the other. For example, because this term "man," which signifies many men, is predicated of the names of individual men, it does not follow that those names which are predicated of the term "man" without a universal sign should be predicated of each other reciprocally.

Similarly, this is [an instance of] the fallacy of accident, because of a similar rule "this spiration is paternity; this spiration is filiation; therefore, filiation is paternity." Similarly, this: "this essence is the Father; this essence is the Son; therefore, the Son is the Father." Similarly this: "this essence is the Father; the Son is not the Father; therefore, the Son is not the essence." Similarly, this: "every God is the Father; the Son is God; therefore, the Son is the Father."

And if it is said that this is not a fallacy because the statement "every God is the Father" is false, an argument can be made against it, because if "every God is the Father" is false, then its opposite, "some God is not the Father," is true. And it is evident that this is true: "some God is the Father"; therefore, there are many gods, of which one is the Father and another is not the Father, just as it follows [that] "some divine essence is the Father; and some divine essence is not the Father; therefore, there are many essences."

Similarly, this is [an instance of] the fallacy of accident: "contradictories are verified of the essence and of the Father; and the essence and the Father are the same; therefore, contradictories are verified of the essence and of the Father for the same thing." Similarly, this is [an instance of] the fallacy of accident: "the essence is the Father; the Father is not the Son; therefore, the essence is not the Son." And for all such [cases], only this rule may be given: the divine essence, which is one God and one single essence, is multiple persons. On which account, where no opposition of the relation prevents it, what is conceded of one person must be conceded of the other; but where opposition of the relation prevents it, what is conceded of one person must not be conceded of any other. And this [rule] must always be observed when responding to discourses involving terms signifying divine persons. And therefore, although the fallacy of accident occurs in such discourses, as exemplified above, nevertheless it never occurs in discourses involving terms signifying creatures. In terms, however, and in discourses involving terms signifying divine persons, the fallacy of accident occurs. But it is otherwise with discourses involving terms signifying creatures and with the discourses already exemplified above.

Wherefore, I say that with respect to terms signifying creatures, wherever the premises are arranged according to the word[43] in mood and in figure, according to the rules mentioned above regarding syllogisms both uniform and mixed, the fallacy of accident never occurs, although there may sometimes be the fallacy of equivocation, amphibology, composition and division, accent, and in one case the fallacy of *secundum quid et simpliciter*, unless certain terms equally include some syncategoremata or certain other qualifications, as discussed in the first treatise of this *Summa*. For this reason, all syllogisms such as the following are valid: "every human intellect is an intellective soul; every human will is an intellective soul; therefore, some human will is a human intellect." "Every creature is created; every creation is a creature; therefore, every creation is created," and innumerable others, which some people, ignorant of logic, deny, for

---

[43]according to the word: *vocaliter* in Latin.

which they lapse into various errors.

But just as sometimes the fallacy of accident occurs because assertoric premises and those in the present [tense] are not arranged according to the due rules in mood and in figure, so too the fallacy of accident occurs because premises in the preterite or future [tense], or of a [particular] modality, do not agree with the true rules in mood and in figure. For which reason, this is [an instance of] the fallacy of accident: "the Son of God was God from eternity; the Son of God was not man from eternity; therefore, man was not the Son of God from eternity." Similarly, this: "God cannot perform a meritorious act without a will; a meritorious act is something; therefore, something cannot be performed by God without a will." Similarly, this: "it can be known naturally that every God is immortal; the three persons are God, or the Father is God; therefore, it can be known naturally that the three persons are immortal, or that the Father is immortal." Similarly, according to one opinion, there is this: "I know that every intellective soul is a substance; the intellect is an intellective soul; therefore, I know that the intellect is a substance." And just as with such cases, so too with many others, which nevertheless, although they can be known evidently, by established rules about the generation of both uniform and mixed syllogisms, many [people] are deceived by the fallacy of accident on account of their ignorance.

The second principal mode of the fallacy of accident occurs when some things are joined through predication to a third, unvaried [thing] in different propositions, and in the conclusion those same things are joined to that same unvaried [thing]; for example, by arguing thus: "this dog is yours; this dog is a father; therefore, this dog is your father."

But it is not always the case, when thus argued, that the fallacy of accident is involved. For this is not [an instance of] the fallacy of accident: "this man is white; this man is an animal; therefore, this man is a white animal." And therefore, in order to know in these sorts of argument when there is the fallacy of accident and when there is not, it must be determined whether, from a proposition in which those two [terms] are conjointly predicated of something, the predication of the one can be inferred from the other, or whether such a statement is [even] proper. And if it is, there is no fallacy of accident. Because this is not [an instance of] the fallacy of accident: "Socrates is rational; Socrates is an animal; therefore, Socrates is a rational animal." If, however, a statement were improper, then it is invalid, just as this does not follow: "Socrates is an animal; Socrates is a man; therefore, Socrates is a man-animal." Nor does this follow: "Socrates is a stone; Socrates is a man; therefore, Socrates is a man-stone." Similarly, if from a proper predication it is impossible to infer the predication of one of the conjoined terms from the other, [then] it is the fallacy of accident. And therefore, because the following consequent is invalid: "he is your father; therefore, he is yours," the following is [an instance of] the fallacy of accident: "this dog is yours; this dog is a father; therefore, this dog is your father." Similarly, because this is invalid: "this is a white monk; therefore, he is white," the following is [an instance of] the fallacy of accident: "this [man] is white; this

[man] is a monk; therefore, this [man] is a white monk," and similarly for consimilar cases.

But it should be known that there is always the fallacy of figure of speech in such an argument, and thus, in such modes of argumentation, there is always the concurrence of the fallacy of accident and the fallacy of figure of speech. Nevertheless, if anyone believes that the conclusion is valid because they [the major and minor terms] were joined with the same third [middle term] in the premises, then he is deceived by the fallacy of accident. If, however, he should believe that the conclusion follows because of the similarity of those expressions to other expressions in which he knows that such a manner of arguing holds [true], he is deceived by the fallacy of figure of speech. And in this case, a certain ambiguity can be attributed to the fallacy of figure of speech, in that one term is understood differently in one proposition than in the other; but, because no single statement is ambiguous, it is neither equivocation, nor amphibology, nor composition and division, nor accent.

Hence, it should be understood that if every term in such a mode of argumentation were always taken uniformly, there would not be any fallacy of speech; indeed, if the syllogistic form were maintained, by not including the middle term in the conclusion, there would not be the fallacy of accident. For example, this is not the fallacy of accident: "this dog is yours; this dog is a father; therefore, some father is yours"; nor is this: "this [man] is white; this [man] is a monk; therefore, some monk is white." But in such a mode of arguing, a certain term is taken differently in different propositions. Hence, in this [proposition]: "this dog is yours," the "yours" signifies possession, but in this one: "this dog is your father," the "your" does not signify possession but rather the father of that man; consequently, it is understood differently in one proposition than in another. But no statement has multiple meanings.

And if you asked, how is it that a term signifies [something] in one proposition and [something else] in another, it must be said that the reason for this can only be [due to] the will of the users, who want to employ [it] in this way.

But from this it seems that this is precisely [an instance of] the fallacy [of figure] of speech. [Yet] it may be said that this is not precisely [an instance of] the fallacy [of figure] of speech because there is nothing inappropriate in supposing that such a mode of arguing might be preserved in mental propositions. Consequently, there is nothing inappropriate in some expression used conventionally signifying one [thing] when posited *per se* and another [thing] when added to something else, so that the same natural sign naturally signifies one [thing] when posited *per se* and another [thing] when joined to something else, as could be exemplified by many natural [signs].

It must be understood, then, that it is possible not only to argue from every affirmative [proposition], but also from one affirmative and another negative. Hence, this is [an instance of] the fallacy of accident: "This man is not white; this man is a monk; therefore, this man is not a white monk." Similarly, this: "this thing is not yours; this thing is a work; therefore, this thing is not your work." And it is consimilar in other cases.

Chapter 12. On the Fallacy of Affirming the Consequent

Because, according to Aristotle, the fallacy of [affirming the] consequent constitutes a part of the [fallacy of] accident, it makes sense to consider the fallacy of [affirming the] consequent after the fallacy of accident.

And the fallacy of [affirming the] consequent occurs when the antecedent is believed to follow from the consequent just as the consequent follows from the antecedent. So that the apparent cause of this fallacy originates in the similarity of the consequent to the antecedent; and the cause of its non-existence is the difference between the antecedent and the consequent. The fallacy of [affirming the] consequent occurs, then, either by arguing from propositions where one follows from the other and not conversely; or by arguing from one conditional to another conditional in which the opposite of the antecedent of the first conditional is put [as] the antecedent, and the opposite of the consequent of the first conditional is put in place of the consequent. For example, by arguing thus: "if a man runs, an animal runs; therefore, if no man runs, no animal runs." For this is the fallacy of affirming the consequent.

And it is a general rule for every such [case] that when one argues from one conditional to another con-

ditional, in which the opposite of the first antecedent
is put in place of the antecedent, and the opposite of
the consequent in place of the consequent, the fallacy
of affirming the consequent occurs. And it [occurs]
for this rule: although a certain consequent may be
valid, the opposite of the antecedent need not infer the
opposite of the consequent, even though sometimes,
because of the terms, the opposite of the consequent
may follow from the opposite of the antecedent. And
therefore, no more needs to be said about this, because it can clearly be known when this mode occurs
and when it does not, knowing the rule just now giv-
en, and knowing when it is another mode of this fallacy.

Hence, it must be understood that the fallacy of [af-
firming the] consequent is sometimes committed by
arguing enthymematically and other times by arguing
from multiple propositions. If argued from multiple
propositions, [then] for there to be [the fallacy of af-
firming] the consequent, it requires that the consequent infer every proposition posited in the antecedent, and not the other way around. And if it were
argued in figure, then there would always be the fallacy of accident at the same time. And, in general,
when there is the fallacy of [affirming the] consequent even in the enthymeme, and that consequent is
reduced to its due (or expected) figure, if the fallacy
of [affirming the] consequent remains in that discourse composed of propositions arranged in [syllo-
gistic] figure, then there will be not only the fallacy of
[affirming the] consequent, but also the fallacy of accident. And the Philosopher says as much, that [the
fallacy of affirming] the consequent is a part of the

[fallacy of] accident, because wherever there is an arrangement (or disposition) of propositions in figure, if the fallacy of [affirming the] consequent is involved, the fallacy of accident will also be involved, but not the other way around. Hence, this is [an instance of] the fallacy of [affirming the] consequent: "every man is an animal; every ass is an animal; therefore, every ass is a man," because both premises follow from the conclusion and not the other way around; and it is also the fallacy of accident, as has been made clear earlier. But here, "every man is white; every man is seen; therefore, everything seen is white" is [an instance of] the fallacy of accident, but it is not [an instance of] the fallacy of [affirming the] consequent, because the conclusion infers neither premise. And therefore, it is false what some [people] say, that arguing from every affirmative [statement] in the second figure always causes the fallacy of [affirming the] consequent.

So, when arguing enthymematically about the fallacy of [affirming the] consequent, it must be observed that generally it will be easy to tell when the fallacy occurs, whether [it is] argued from multiple premises or not.

Hence, it should be known that, in order to attribute the fallacy of [affirming the] consequent, it is not enough to say that the inference proceeds in the opposite direction and not vice versa. For although this is the general explanation, nevertheless in addition to this general explanation it is necessary to give another specific rule as to why it proceeds in the opposite direction and not vice versa. And this consists in assigning two specific rules, in one of which it is declared that [the argument] follows from the converse, and in the other not. And thus, in general, when attributing the fallacy of [affirming the] consequent [to an argument], two specific rules must be given, and for different sophisms different rules need to be employed, some examples of which will follow.

Hence, it must be understood that when the argument proceeds distributively from an inferior to a superior term, it is [an instance of] the fallacy of [affirming the] consequent. For example, this is [an example of] the fallacy of [affirming the] consequent: "every man runs; therefore, every animal runs." For it holds [valid] in the converse [direction] according to this rule: "[proceeding] distributively from the superior to the inferior [term], the conclusion is valid"; but it does not hold in this [the opposite] direction, because [when proceeding] distributively from the inferior to the superior [term] the consequence is not valid.

Similarly, when arguing from a term suppositing merely confusedly to a term suppositing determinately, with no variation made to the other terms, it is [an instance of] the fallacy of [affirming the] consequent. For example, this is [an instance of] the fallacy of [affirming the] consequent: "every man is an animal, therefore, an animal is every man." For it holds from the converse, according to this rule: "from a term suppositing determinately to a term suppositing merely confusedly, [provided] no variation is made with respect to the other terms, the consequence is valid," in that it is possible to ascend to the term suppositing merely confusedly. But it does not hold in the following way, on account of the rule just now mentioned, namely, that "from a term suppositing merely confusedly to a term suppositing determinately, the consequent is invalid."

Hence, in this way, the sophisms that follow are all in error: "for every part of this continuum, some part of it was previously terminated; therefore, some part of this continuum was previously terminated for every part of this continuum"; "between every future instant and this instant there is some intermediate instant; therefore, some instant is intermediate between every future instant and this instant"; "from every quantity some greater quantity can be made; therefore, some greater quantity can be made from every quantity"; "after every day, some day can be; therefore, some day can be after every day"; "from every part of a whole some lesser part can be given; therefore, some lesser part can be given from every part of a whole." For in all these and consimilar [cases], the predicate supposits merely confusedly in the antecedent because it mediately follows the sign, and it supposits determinately in the conclusion because it precedes the sign; therefore, it is [an instance of] the fallacy of [affirming the] consequent. Similarly, there is this: "both of them can be true, now that the two doubtful contradictories have been demonstrated; therefore, something true there can be about both of them."

Likewise, when arguing from a term suppositing determinately or merely confusedly to a term suppositing confusedly and distributively, there is the fallacy of [affirming the] consequent. Just as with this: "you are ignorant about some proposition; therefore, you

do not know some proposition"; "you doubt something; therefore, you do not know something";
"Socrates sees a non-man; therefore, Socrates does
not see a man."

Likewise, when [terms in] the oblique and nominative
[cases] follow a universal affirmative sign, first by
placing the nominative after the sign and the oblique,
and later placing the nominative before the sign and
the oblique, it is [an instance of] the fallacy of [af-
firming the] consequent. For example, by arguing
thus: "every man an ass is the seer of; therefore, the
seer of every man is an ass"; because it posits that
some ass sees some man, and that no ass sees every
man, therefore the antecedent is true, and the consequent false.

Likewise, when each singular [instance] of some universal [proposition] is taken to be true *per se*, but
when taken altogether they are incompatible, and yet
each is compatible with the other [when taken sepa-
rately]; then, when arguing from the universal [propo-
sition] about [what is] possible, for an equivalent
sense of composition, to a proposition about [what is]
possible when a subject with the same sign is placed
on the side of the predicate, it is [an instance of] the
fallacy of [affirming the] consequent. For example,
by arguing thus: "according to every sign, a continuum can be divided; therefore, a continuum can be divided according to every sign." Nor does it follow
that "a continuum can be divided according to this
sign, and a continuum can be divided according to
that sign, and so on for each singular [instance];
therefore, a continuum can be divided according to

every sign." However, one such proposition is frequently posited by authors in place of another, although by strength of expression they are not equivalent. On account of which, in such cases, there is the fallacy of [affirming the] consequent, according to Aristotle's principles: "of every form this matter can be deprived; therefore, this matter can be deprived of every form." For by this [proposition] "of every form this matter can be deprived," it is denoted that each [proposition] such as the following is possible: "of this form this matter is deprived," for any form indicated. And it is clear, according to Aristotle's principles, that each such [a proposition] is true. But by this [proposition]: "this matter can be deprived of every form," what is denoted is that the following is possible: "this matter is deprived of every form." But this is impossible, according to Aristotle's principles.

Similarly, this is [an instance of] the fallacy of [affirming the] consequent: "in each future instant he can sin," pointing to someone who is now [engaged] in a meritorious act; "therefore, this man can sin in each future instant." For the antecedent is true and the consequent false, in that a last [moment] of being cannot be granted to a permanent thing, and consequently, if he is [engaged] in a meritorious act, he will [continue to] exist after that instant.

Similarly, this is [an instance of] the fallacy of [affirming the] consequent: "before each future instant, Socrates is able not to exist; therefore, Socrates is able not to exist before each future instant."

Likewise, when some modal proposition cannot be converted by precisely transposing the terms following and preceding a word or words, [then] arguing from such an indefinite or universal modal [proposition] to a specific converse or its equivalent is [an instance of] the fallacy of [affirming the] consequent, insofar as it [the error] arises from the form of reasoning, although in some ways it may hold. For this reason, there is the fallacy of [affirming the] consequent in such [propositions]: "a meritorious act God can perform alone [without help from others]; therefore, God alone [and nobody else] can perform a meritorious act."

That said, it should be understood that, in all such previously mentioned [cases], the fallacy can be ascribed to figure of speech.

Many other rules can be given for this fallacy. But it should be understood that, in order to know in general when the fallacy of [affirming the] consequent occurs and when it does not, one needs to understand all the rules previously stated with respect to the consequents, as well as all those in general that may apply to any enthymeme whatsoever. And, therefore, unless all the rules about consequents are known, it is not always possible to know when this fallacy occurs and when it does not.

Chapter 13: On the Fallacy of *Secundum Quid et Simpliciter*

What follows is a discussion of the fallacy of *secundum quid et simpliciter*, which occurs when an argument proceeds sophistically from something taken with a qualification to something taken *per se*, or vice versa.

The reason for the appearance of this fallacy is the similarity of something taken *per se* to the same thing taken with something else. The reason for its non-existence is their difference.

It is necessary to know, however, that *secundum quid* here refers to a term taken with the addition [of something else], whereas *simpliciter* refers to a term taken *per se*, without such an addition.

Moreover, there are two principal modes of this fallacy. The first mode is when the argument proceeds from being *secundum adiacens,* to the same thing when it is *tertium adiacens*, whether affirmatively or negatively. The second mode is when, from part of the same extreme, the argument proceeds from something taken with an addition, to [the thing] itself, or [to] its superior or a convertible [term] without addition, or conversely.

According to the first [principal] mode, sophisms such as the following are in error: "the Antichrist does not exist; therefore, the Antichrist is not possible"; "the Antichrist does not exist; therefore, the Antichrist is not known by you." Now, in the second argument, there is no fallacy of [affirming the] consequent because the converse does not follow, even though in the first argument there is both the fallacy of [affirming the] consequent and the fallacy of *secundum quid et simpliciter*. The fallacy of *secundum quid et simpliciter* is there because the argument proceeds from [a term] taken *per se* to the same [term] taken together with the following predicate, which predicate can thus agree with the term suppositing for a non-entity just as [it can] for an entity. And whenever it is argued in this way, there is the fallacy of *secundum quid et simpliciter* when arguing negatively and, conversely, when arguing affirmatively. Just as this is [an instance of] the fallacy of *secundum quid et simpliciter:* "*a* is producible by God; therefore, *a* exists," and similarly this: "*a* does not exist; therefore, *a* is not producible by God." Similarly this: "the Antichrist does not exist; therefore, the Antichrist is not foreknown by God," and conversely: "the Antichrist is foreknown by God; therefore, the Antichrist exists." Hence, because that which does not exist can be foreknown just as that which does, there is the fallacy of *secundum quid et simpliciter* in such [arguments]. And this is one general rule for this mode of the fallacy. But knowing in particular when a predicate may agree with a term [suppositing] for a non-entity as well as for an entity does not belong strictly to the logician, but it does belong to someone who knows logic and other particular sciences.

Another rule for this mode [of fallacy] is that, when a

predicate is not common to all [its superiors], there is always the fallacy of *secundum quid et simpliciter* when arguing affirmatively or negatively. For example, here is [an instance of] the fallacy of *secundum quid et simpliciter*: "Socrates is not an ass; therefore, Socrates does not exist"; and "a man exists; therefore, a man is an ass." Hence, in general, when argued negatively, it is the fallacy of *secundum quid et simpliciter*. Similarly, when arguing affirmatively from the consequent, it is the fallacy of *secundum quid et simpliciter*.

The second principal mode is when, from part of the same extreme, the argument proceeds from something taken with an addition, to [the thing] itself, or [to] its superior or a convertible [term], taken *per se*, or conversely. And then it must be seen whether what is added, and that to which it is added, are construed as an adjective and substantive or not. If the former, either the predication of the one about the other is impossible, or the predication of the one about the other, taken universally, is necessary or contingent. If that be impossible, always arguing affirmatively from such [a thing] taken with another [thing added] to itself, or [to a] convertible [term], [then] there is the fallacy of *secundum quid et simpliciter*, but not always when arguing to whatever is its superior [term].[44] For example, this is [an instance of] the fallacy of *secundum quid et simpliciter:* "Socrates is a dead man; therefore, Socrates is a man," because this is impossible: "a man is dead." Similarly, by the same [logic], this is [an instance of] the fallacy of *secundum quid et simpliciter:* "Socrates is a dead man;

---

[44]superior: i.e., more general term.

therefore, Socrates is either rational or risible." Similarly, this: "*a* is a sophistical syllogism; therefore, *a* is a syllogism," because this is impossible: "some syllogism is sophistical." Similarly, this: "this is a false argument; therefore, this is an argument." Similarly, this: "he is a good brigand; therefore, he is good." Similarly, this: "he is the perfect brigand; therefore, he is perfect."

However, although it is the fallacy of *secundum quid et simpliciter* [when arguing] with respect to one part, it is not always the fallacy of *secundum quid et simpliciter* when arguing the other way around. For example, this is not [an instance of] the fallacy: "Socrates is a dead man; therefore, Socrates is dead." Nor this: "Socrates is a perfect brigand, therefore he is a brigand." Nor this: "he is a good cobbler; therefore, he is a cobbler." Nor this: "*a* is a sophistical syllogism, therefore *a* is sophistical."

However, in order to know to which part the argument proceeds when there is the fallacy of *secundum quid et simpliciter,* and to which it does not, there needs to be a definition of the entire composite, or some term convertible with it, by employing a nominal definition. And if in that definition one part is put affirmatively, or something convertible with one part and not with another, [then] always arguing with respect to that part is a valid argument, whereas arguing to the other is [an instance of] the fallacy of *secundum quid et simpliciter.* For example, let this entire [expression] "dead man," or some other term convertible with it, be defined. And such a definition will be given "that it is not a man, but was a man." Here, "man" is put negatively; therefore, when arguing with respect to man it is [an instance of] the fallacy of *secundum quid et simpliciter,* but when arguing with respect to another part it is a valid argument. Similarly, let this entire expression, "perfect brigand," or some noun convertible with it, be defined, and it will be said that a "brigand is someone who knows the art of brigandage perfectly." Here, "brigand" and not "perfect," nor any term convertible with perfect, is asserted; and therefore, the following is not [an instance of] the fallacy of *secundum quid et simpliciter:* "he is a perfect brigand; therefore, he is a brigand," whereas the following is an instance of the fallacy of *secundum quid et simpliciter:* "he is a perfect brigand; therefore, he is perfect." Similarly, a good cobbler is a cobbler perfectly knowledgeable in the art of sewing; therefore, the following is not an instance of the fallacy of *secundum quid et simpliciter:* "he is a good cobbler; therefore, he is a cobbler," but this is: "he is a good cobbler; therefore, he is good." And just as it is said of these, so must it be said of others [like them]. For if some term were convertible with the entire expression "white monk," it would need to be defined in this way: "a monk wearing the white vestment of his profession." And for this reason, the following is not an instance of the fallacy of *secundum quid et simpliciter:* "he is a white monk; therefore, he is a monk," but this is: "he is a white monk; therefore, he is white."

If, however, the predication of one part, or the entirety of the other, is necessary, [then] it is always valid to argue with respect to either part without any fallacy, at least in creatures. Perhaps in divine things, on account of something proper to God, who is one simple essence and three persons, such a mode of arguing is not valid: "the essence is a generative Father; therefore, the essence is generative." If, however, the predication of one part, or the entirety of the other, is contingent, then that skill must be employed which expresses the definition of some noun convertible with the whole. And if both parts are included in that definition, or something convertible with both parts, [then] it is always a valid argument without fallacy [that proceeds] from the whole to each part. For example, if a certain noun were convertible with the whole [expression] "a white man" and its ultimate nominal definition ought to be defined, [then] it ought to be defined in this way: "a man having whiteness." And here "man" is posited, and there "having whiteness" is posited, which is convertible with "white," and therefore it follows that "Socrates is a white man; therefore, Socrates is a man and Socrates is white." But if both parts, or something convertible [with them], are not ultimately posited in such a nominal definition, but only one [part is], then for the one [part] it would be [an instance of] the fallacy of *secundum quid et simpliciter* but not for the other.

And by this rule it is clear that the following arguments do not err on account of the fallacy of *secundum quid et simpliciter:* "a white man is an aggregate *per accidens*; therefore, a man is an aggregate *per accidens*"; "a stone is considered eternal; therefore, a stone is eternal"; "Caesar is opinable; therefore, Caesar is," and the like. But in such [arguments] and others like them, a certain ambiguity may be attributed [to them] on account of equivocation and amphibology; in one sense the consequences will be valid, and in another they will not.

The things just discussed must be understood when the argument proceeds affirmatively from such [terms]. From which it may easily be seen what must be said about them when the argument proceeds negatively, because when, by arguing affirmatively, there is the fallacy of *secundum quid et simpliciter*, [then] by arguing negatively from the opposite [direction] of the consequent, there will likewise be the fallacy of *secundum quid et simpliciter*.

But if the addition, and that to which it is added, do not act as an adjective and a substantive, then either the whole [formed] from the addition, and that to which it is added, may indiscriminately serve as the predicate and subject of a proposition, – as the following examples illustrate: "white in the teeth," "the understanding of a rock," "the servant of a man," and so on – or they may not. If they do, it must be seen whether the part is necessarily predicated of the whole, – given a constancy posited of the subject, which may be known by its nominal definition – or whether it is not. But if it is, then an argument proceeding from the whole to the part is valid; and it easily follows that "the understanding of a stone is prior to the Son; therefore, the understanding is prior to the Son." Similarly, it easily follows that "the understanding by which God understands a stone is posterior to the Father; therefore, the understanding of creation is posterior to the Father." Similarly, the following consequent is valid: "the understanding by which God understands creation is posterior to the Father;

therefore, the understanding by which God understands is posterior to the Father." And therefore, just
as the consequent is false, so too is the antecedent. On
account of which the following propositions are false:
"the understanding of creation presupposes a divine
suppositum"; "the understanding of creation presupposes the emanation of persons"; "a person presupposes an understanding of creation"; "a person presupposes an essence," and so forth.

If, however, it is not necessary that the whole be predicated of a part, nor vice versa, even while the subject
remains constant, [then an argument] always [pro-
ceeding] from such [a term] with the addition, to the
same [term] taken *per se,* is an instance of the fallacy
of *secundum quid et simpliciter.* For example:
"[something] white in the teeth runs; therefore,
[something] white runs"; "this is your father; therefore, he is yours"; "this is your work; therefore, it is
yours."

But in order to know when such a fallacy occurs, and
when, by not reasoning in such a manner, it does not,
it is useful to resolve propositions into prior ones, as
much as possible, – either by expressing nominal definitions, or by some other suitable means, – and to determine from the propositions into which a resolution
is made whether such a mode of argumentation is
valid. For example, this proposition: "an Ethiopian is
white in the teeth" is equivalent to this one: "an
Ethiopian has white teeth"; and, therefore, it is clear
that the following is not valid: "an Ethiopian has
white teeth; therefore, he is white," nor is this one:
"an Ethiopian is white in the teeth; therefore, he is

white."

It is necessary to understand, however, that the afore-mentioned [statements] apply to purely categorical propositions, which are not equivalent to conditional ones, because such consequences are not always valid in such [propositions], even though a part is predicated of the whole. For this reason, such a mode of arguing from some expressions is not valid, but from others it is. Hence, the following is valid: "Socrates is in the dirt with a hundred marks; therefore, Socrates is in the dirt." And yet, the following is not valid: "Socrates would like to be in the dirt with a hundred marks; therefore, Socrates would like to be in the dirt." For this [proposition]: "Socrates is in the dirt with a hundred marks" is not equivalent to any conditional one, but this [proposition]: "Socrates would like to be in the dirt with a hundred marks" is equivalent to this conditional [proposition]: "Socrates would like to be in the dirt if he could earn a hundred marks by it." Similarly, the following consequent is valid: "I do not sell you a horse; therefore, I do not sell you a horse for one hundred marks"; and yet, this does not follow: "I would not like to sell you a horse; therefore, I would not like to sell you a horse for a hundred marks."

If, however, that which is added, and that to which it is added, cannot indiscriminately be the subject or the predicate of a proposition, then what is added is an adverb, or a proposition with its causality, or something similar. For which reason, it is difficult, if not impossible, to give a general rule appropriate to such [cases] and in such [matters], because sometimes the fallacy of *secundum quid et simpliciter* occurs when arguing negatively from a determinable with an addition, to [the thing] itself taken *per se*, and sometimes the fallacy *secundum quid et simpliciter* occurs when arguing affirmatively. For example, these are [instances of] the fallacy of *secundum quid et simpliciter:* "a man is not necessarily an animal; therefore, a man is not an animal"; "God was not always creating; therefore, God was not creating"; "man does not run quickly; therefore, man does not run." Likewise, when arguing affirmatively, the fallacy of *secundum quid et simpliciter* occurs when the argument in such [cases] proceeds from something taken *per se* to the same thing taken with such a determination [i.e., a qualification], as in the following example: "a man is an animal; therefore, a man is necessarily an animal."

But it is necessary to understand, with respect to this fallacy, that when it is argued from something taken with a determination to the same thing taken *per se*, or vice versa, the proposition, by which such a consequent is expressed and reduced into a syllogism, must be accepted; and it must be seen whether that proposition, or the conditional corresponding to that categorical, is necessary or not. If it is, it is not an instance of the fallacy of *secundum quid et simpliciter.* If neither that categorical [proposition] nor the corresponding conditional [one] is necessary, then it is the fallacy of *secundum quid et simpliciter.* For example, if it is argued that "Socrates is white with respect to his foot; therefore, Socrates is white," then the following proposition must be added [to it]: "every white thing with respect to its foot is white," by which, once expressed, the syllogistic form is complete, thus arguing that "anything white with respect to its foot is white; Socrates is white with respect to his foot; therefore, Socrates is white." And if the following proposition, or the conditional [one], be necessary – "if anything is white with respect to its foot, it is white" – [then] the first consequence will be valid. But because neither of those propositions is necessary, there is the fallacy of *secundum quid et simpliciter* in both of them. And it is consimilar with others.

Chapter 14. On the Fallacy of Irrelevant Conclusion[45]

Something remains to be said now about the fallacy of irrelevant conclusion, which is a deception arising from the absence of any of the four particular phrases: "[in reference] to the same [thing]," "with respect to the same [thing]," "in the same way [or similarly]," and "at the same time."

To clarify, it must be understood that these particular phrases are not to be included in the refutation, and that propositions must be adopted whose form gives no indication of a verification made with their negation, namely, in reference to different things, or with respect to different things, or in a different way [dissimilarly], or at a different time; but when the form of a proposition gives an indication of any of these [negations], it is [an instance of] the fallacy of irrelevant conclusion.

And this fallacy can occur in four ways, according to the four particular phrases. One way, because the expressions are with respect to different things, is this: "this is the double of a; and this is not the double of b; therefore, this is the double and not the double." Likewise, "Socrates is similar to Plato; Socrates is not similar to John; therefore, Socrates is similar and not similar." Similarly, this: "Socrates is the son of Plato;

---

[45]irrelevant conclusion: or irrelevant refutation (*ignoratio elenchi*).

Socrates is not the son of Cicero; therefore, Socrates is the son and not the son."

The second way [this fallacy can occur], namely, "with respect to the same [thing]," is illustrated in the following paralogisms: "Socrates is similar to Plato with respect to whiteness; Socrates is not similar to Plato with respect to music; therefore, Socrates is similar and not similar to Plato." Similarly, this: "a is the double of b in terms of length; a is not the double of b in terms of width; therefore a with respect to b is the double and not the double." The [fallacy of] irrelevant conclusion can even occur like this: "a is the double of b; a is not wider than b; therefore, a is, with respect to b, the double and not the double."

The third way is illustrated in the following paralogisms: "Socrates runs quickly; Socrates does not necessarily run; therefore, Socrates runs and does not run." Similarly, this: "this man disputes knowledgeably; this man does not dispute unwillingly; therefore, this man disputes and does not dispute."

The fourth way is illustrated in paralogisms such as the following: "this man will run tomorrow; this man will not run after tomorrow; therefore, this man will run and will not run." Similarly, this: "Christ was God from eternity [out of time]; and he was a man in time; therefore, he was a man and was not a man."

And every aforementioned sophism errs because the aforementioned verification occurs in them in reference to different things, or with respect to different things, or in a different way, or at a different time.

It must be understood, however, that in such a way of

arguing, either a contradiction of incomplex [terms] is inferred, as the examples have shown, and in that case the discourse is simply invalid; or contradictory incomplex [terms] happen to be introduced, but then the discourse is still invalid by virtue of the expression, even though, according to the usage of some, the conclusions would need to be considered invalid. Now, the contradictory incomplex [terms] are not inferred about the same [thing], but about things that are relative opposites, and in that case the argument can absolutely be granted without fallacy. Just as the following illustrates: "Socrates is similar to Plato; Socrates is dissimilar to Cicero; therefore, Socrates is similar and dissimilar."

Similarly, in the fourth way [that this fallacy may occur], it is possible to infer contradictory incomplex [terms], by arguing thus: "Socrates will be white in *a* [measure of time]; Socrates will be non-white in *b* [measure of time]; therefore, Socrates will be white and not white." But it does not follow that "Socrates will be white and not white; therefore, Socrates will be white and will not be white," because the following consequence is invalid: "Socrates will be non-white; therefore, Socrates will not be white." However, if the argument were made using a present-tense verb, the consequence would be valid. In that case, there can be [the fallacy of] irrelevant conclusion without the fallacy of *secundum quid et simpliciter*; and yet, wherever [the fallacy of] irrelevant conclusion occurs, there is often [also] the fallacy of *secundum quid et simpliciter*, because then it frequently happens that the argument proceeds sophistically from something taken with an addition, to [the thing] itself taken *per se*, and consequently the fallacy of *secundum quid et simpliciter* occurs.

Chapter 15. On the Fallacy of *Petitio Principii*[46]

After [having discussed] fallacies in which faulty arguments err in form, something must be said about fallacies in which sophistical arguments do not err, but in which the opponent errs when arguing against the respondent. The first of these [fallacies] is [that of] *petitio principii*, which occurs when the opponent, although he may infer the conclusion that he intends, nevertheless he cannot convince the respondent, because he accepts what he ought to prove instead. And it is called [the fallacy of] "*petitio principii*," not because he accepts the very thing that he ought to infer, for then there would be no appearance [of reasoning on his part], but [because] the opponent is said to beg the question when he accepts something equally unknown, or more unknown, than what he ought to infer. And for this reason, the respondent may always ask for proof of the assumption until he accepts something more known.

Moreover, this fallacy occurs in many ways. One way is when the argument proceeds from a synonymous noun to a synonym; for example, when arguing like this: "Marcus runs; therefore, Tullius runs." For, immediately, something equally unknown is accepted as the conclusion that must be inferred.

---

[46] *petitio principii*: also known as "begging the question."

Another way [in which this fallacy may occur] is when the argument proceeds from a nominal definition to the thing defined, or vice versa. And this is because in every disputation the signification of the words must be presupposed. Hence, the following appears to be [an instance of the fallacy of] *petitio principii*: "fire is productive of calories [heat]; therefore, fire is calefactive."

Another way [in which this fallacy may occur] is when the argument proceeds from one convertible[47] proposition to another, neither of which is prior or better known than the other; for example: "no musician is a grammarian; therefore, no grammarian is a musician." Hence, in general, whenever [something] is assumed [to be] equally unknown or more unknown to its respondent than the conclusion [that] is to be inferred, it is [an instance of the fallacy of] *petitio principii*.

Nevertheless, it must be understood that although the respondent may not be convinced by reason so long as [something] equally unknown or more unknown is accepted, he may still be convinced by authority if he is willing to accept authority. For example, if the respondent, reluctant to deny a certain authority, were to deny that "Marcus runs," even though the opponent argues that "Tullius runs; therefore, Marcus runs," he [the opponent] would not convince him; but if he states that "Tullius runs" on [the basis of] an authority that he is not willing to deny, he will sufficiently convince him. And so it is in other cases.

---

[47]convertible: equivalent.

Chapter 16. On the Fallacy of False Cause[48]

After [the fallacy of] *petitio principii* comes the fallacy of false cause, in which a certain paralogism errs in form only if the conclusion does not follow from the antecedent, unless some other fallacy impedes the illation.

In evidence of which, it must be understood that the fallacy of false cause is only [to be found] in syllogisms leading to the impossible, that is, to what is false with respect either to the truth or to the response or opinion of the respondent. And it occurs in those syllogisms of false cause when, from the impossibility or falseness of a conclusion, something is inferred to be false which, once posited, that is, as being false or true, the false conclusion nonetheless still follows, so that whether the assumption was true or false, the conclusion will always remain false; and, therefore, the fallacy of false cause coincides with "not on this account is it false," which Aristotle defines in Book II of his *Prior Analytics*.

There are, however, two modes of this fallacy. One [mode] is when a certain proposition, superfluous even to the illation, is taken [to be true] and appears to be the cause of the conclusion's falsity, even if the conclusion is not false on account of it. For example, if the following proposition were given: "the soul and life are really the same thing," and an opponent

---

[48]false cause: or *secundum non-causam ut causam*.

wished to prove it false by leading from it to the impossible by arguing thus: "the soul and life are really the same thing; death and life are opposites, and death is opposite to generation; therefore, life is opposite to corruption." This conclusion is false and, consequently, so is "the soul and life are really the same" from which the falsity follows. This is the fallacy of false cause because the conclusion that "life is opposite to corruption" nonetheless follows whether "the soul and life are really the same" is true or not.

The second mode of this fallacy is when a proposition superfluous to the illation of falsehood is not accepted [as true], but the conclusion is not false on account of the proposition's falsehood. For example, if a respondent were to assert the proposition that "no white thing is black is necessary" and an opponent wished to prove it false by deducing an impossibility from it and arguing thus: "everything that proceeds from whiteness to blackness is partly white and partly black because it belongs partly to whiteness and partly to blackness; [that] no white thing is black is necessary; therefore, it is necessary [that] nothing proceeds from whiteness to blackness." This conclusion is false, therefore the proposition from which it follows, "[that] no white thing is black is necessary," is [also] false. It should be noted that the false conclusion does not result from the falsity in the minor premise, "[that] no white thing is black is necessary," but rather from the falsity in the major premise that "everything that proceeds from whiteness to blackness is partly white and partly black."

Hence, it should be understood that the response in

this case is that the impossible conclusion is arrived at not on account of the impossibility of a pre-concession, but on account of the impossibility of a co-assumption. But sometimes an impossibility results not on account of the impossibility of a pre-concession nor on account of the impossibility of a co-assumption, but on account of the incompossibility of the two. For example, if the arguer wanted to prove to the respondent the impossibility of this "you sit" by arguing the following instead: "you sit; you stand; therefore, the contradictory statements and true at the same time. The conclusion is impossible, and 'you stand' is possible; therefore, 'you sit' is impossible." It must be remarked that this impossible conclusion does not follow, neither on account of the impossibility of the one, nor on account of the impossibility of the other, but on account of their incompossibility.

And it is in this way that such sophisms are resolved: if the respondent were to say "it is possible for him to be damned" by indicating someone who is actually predestined, and the opponent were to prove it false, like this: "if this be true [that] 'it is possible for him to be damned,' let it be posited." Once posited, an impossibility follows: "he is predestined; he is damned; therefore, a damned man is predestined." The conclusion is impossible, and the major [premise] is true or indeterminately true; therefore, the minor [premise] is impossible; and consequently the statement "it is possible for him to be damned" is false. It must be replied that an impossible conclusion follows, not because [the statement] "it is possible for him to be damned" is false, nor because that same statement is posited [as true], but because two incompossible propositions occur in the antecedent.

So it must be understood that although the first argument, which has a false or impossible conclusion,
does not err in form or in substance, nevertheless,
upon further analysis, when it is argued that "the conclusion is false; and not the premise; but the remain-
der" or that "the conclusion is false; therefore, the
conceded assumption is false" – there is an error in either the form or the substance; as a result, the consequence is invalid according to the truth or according
to the respondent's response, assuming he responded
correctly, or some proposition that he accepts as true
is false.

Chapter 17. On the Fallacy of Many Questions

The final fallacy is the fallacy of many questions. It entails a certain argument that does not err so much in the illation as in the opponent arguing against the respondent, because he treats one question which [actually] turns out to be many, that is, which is equivalent to many [questions]. From which, if he later argues sophistically, his argument will err for some other fallacy. If, however, [once] a question [is] asked, the respondent immediately responds with a single response, he could easily be deceived, and therefore this fallacy is to be counted among the [other] fallacies.

It should be realized, however, that a certain question can be understood as multiple questions, in two ways: either many [things] are asserted of many [subjects], or one thing [is asserted] of many [subjects] or vice versa; or the terms are taken to be singular in number so that, nonetheless, the proposition from which such a question is formed is a proposition of one unity sufficient for contradiction.

Alternatively, a question can be multiple [questions] because the statement is not one. For example, by saying this: "Socrates is a man-ass" or "Socrates is a musical, white, hot grammarian."

To the question that is multiple [questions] in the first

way [mentioned earlier], one response can always be given, by conceding or negating, nor can one be drawn into contradiction by such a response.

For, since one part of a contradiction is always true and the other false, one part must be negated, and the other affirmed. Hence, with two things [proposed], of which one is white and the other black, if someone is asked whether they are both white or black, it ought to be said in response that they are neither white nor black. And it is the same in other cases, that the one part can be affirmed or negated. However, if someone wanted to respond affirmatively in many similar cases, he should not give just one response but many, by saying that this is white and that black, and so forth in consimilar [cases].

To a question which is multiple [questions], in the second way [mentioned earlier], he should not give a single response; but if a respondent wanted to respond, he ought to give multiple responses; so that, if he were asked whether Socrates were a white musician, he ought not to respond by conceding or negating. But if he wanted to respond, he ought to give multiple responses; for example, if Socrates is white and not a musician, he ought to say that he is white and that he is not a musician. And so it must be said in consimilar cases.

Chapter 18. In What Way All Fallacies Err Against the Syllogism

After the foregoing, it remains to be seen how the aforementioned fallacies err against the syllogism and in what way paralogisms, which seem [to be] complete syllogisms but are not, fall short of the nature of a syllogism.

And in fallacies comprising ambiguous propositions, it is not difficult to see this. For such paralogisms are verbally similar to true syllogisms, as is clear from the equivocation in the following paralogisms: "every dog runs; a heavenly constellation is a dog; therefore, a heavenly constellation runs"; "every man is a rational animal; this statue is a man; therefore, this statue is a rational animal"; "no animal is a species; man is a species; therefore, man is not an animal." For these paralogisms are constructed verbally in the same way that perfect syllogisms are constructed; nor is there any defect in the syllogism here except that in each of them there is a proposition that must be distinguished with respect to equivocation.

As for [the fallacy of] amphibology, the paralogisms are constructed as follows: "every true proposition, if it is necessary, is possible; that you are an ass is a true proposition, if it is necessary; therefore, that you are an ass is possible"; "whoever sells oil is a merchant; that sycophant sells oil; therefore, that sycophant is a merchant"; "whatever is [predicated of] one of them and the other of them is [predicated of] both of them; something is true of one of them and the other of them; therefore, something is true of both of them" [whereby] the two contradictories have been demonstrated. In these paralogisms, the true conditions of a syllogism are met except that they contain some proposition that is ambiguous according to amphibology. As for [the fallacy of] composition and division, the paralogisms are constructed as follows: "whoever lives always exists; this man lives; therefore, this man always exists."

As for [the fallacy of] accent, the paralogisms are constructed as follows: "no just person ought to *pendere*; this man is just; therefore, this man ought not to *pendere*."[49]

As for the fallacy of figure of speech, paralogisms are constructed as follows: "every substance is subject to an accident; every animal is a substance; therefore, every animal is subject to an accident";[50] "whatever you bought yesterday, you ate today; you bought raw meat yesterday; therefore, you ate raw meat today."[51]

---

[49]*pendere*: to ponder or consider; but *pendēre*: to hang or be suspended. Thus, the ambiguity.

[50]every substance is subject... every animal is subject...: in Latin, the phrase is "omnis substantia est subiecta... omne animal est subiecta..." The fallacy derives from the use of "subiecta," the singular feminine form of the adjective (in nominative case) with animal, a neuter noun (used in the singular nominative case). In Latin we see it, and the fallacy of the "grammatical accident of words" exists. In English, we don't see it and it doesn't exist.

[51]whatever you bought yesterday: the fallacy of figure of speech in this syllogism is not obvious (in Latin or English); one would

For in these [examples], the syllogistic form is not preserved, as is clear from the previously given rules around the syllogism and its species. Likewise, what follows is the fallacy of figure of speech, failing to meet the conditions of the syllogism: "Anything other than God, God can create without another creature; riding a horse is [something] other than God; therefore, God can create a man riding a horse without a horse."

As for [the fallacy of] accident, [its] paralogisms are constructed as follows: "man runs; Socrates is a man; therefore Socrates runs"; "this dog is yours; this dog is a father; therefore, this dog is your father." For in these paralogisms, and in all paralogisms of [the fallacy of] accident, the proper form of the premises is preserved, but in the first paralogism the mood is not observed, because the premises are not arranged in the proper manner, therefore it is not a syllogism [but a paralogism].[52] In the second paralogism, although the premises are properly arranged, nevertheless the conclusion is not properly inferred from the premises because the major extreme and minor extreme are joined on the side of the same extreme, and the middle term is placed in the conclusion;[53] both of which are at odds with the [proper form of the] syllogism;

---

assume it hinges on the word "whatever" which may be too broad, based on a context that we do not have (but the speaker does). On the surface, it seems like a fallacy of irrelevant conclusion.

[52]the premises are not arranged in the proper manner: presumably because the mood is III, and there is no III in the first figure. But if the major premise were "a man runs" (instead of "man runs") then the mood would be All (Darii) and there would not be a fallacy. See Spade for more on figure and mood.

for this reason, the syllogistic form is not preserved there. And thus, they are not complete syllogisms.

As for the fallacy of [affirming the] consequent, paralogisms are constructed as follows: "every man runs; every man is an animal; therefore, every animal runs." This is indeed a defective syllogism, because a universal conclusion is inferred which ought to be particular.

As for the fallacy of *secundum quid et simpliciter*, paralogisms are formed as follows: "no prudent man wants to enrich his enemy; this man is prudent; therefore, this man would not want to enrich his enemy for the good of the republic." There is no defect here, except that something determinate is added to the conclusion which was not included in the premises, and therefore it is [an instance] of the fallacy of *secundum quid et simpliciter*.

As for the [fallacy of] irrelevant conclusion, paralogisms are formed as follows: having conceded that an Ethiopian is black, it is argued, in order to prove that the Ethiopian is not black, thus: "nothing white is black; the Ethiopian is white in his teeth; therefore, the Ethiopian is not black." Here indeed is a fallacy because, contrary to what the respondent assumes, it is not absolutely accepted that the Ethiopian is white, but [only] that he is white according to some part [of his body] which is not black; but according to some other part [of his body] the Ethiopian is black, and for this reason the argument is not accepted. And thus, it

---

[53]major extreme... minor extreme...: in other words, the "dog" is in the subject position in major, minor and conclusion; and "father" is in the predicate position in minor and conclusion.

is not accepted according to the same [refutation], on account of which, it is [an instance of] the fallacy of irrelevant conclusion.

As for the remaining fallacies, they are not constructed with arguments erring in form, although an opponent may err by employing them when disputing with a respondent; so it is not necessary to give examples of them. Indeed, every apparent argument erring in form errs on account of one of the other [fallacies].

The sufficiency and number of which can be understood as follows: because every paralogism that is vocal, or according to the voice, insofar as the plurality of incomplex [terms] and the quantity and quality of propositions [are concerned], is similar to a true syllogism, which conditions previously posited in the treatise on syllogism correspond to; or they are not similar to a syllogism according to the voice. In the first case, it is impossible for there to be any defect, except as might be owing to the ambiguity or incongruousness of some expression, or because the same term, without ambiguity, supposits for one thing in one proposition and another thing in another. This proposition cannot be demonstrated, but it is accepted by induction.

If a syllogism is invalid owing to the first [case], namely, because there is some ambiguity in it: [then] it is entirely similar to the following syllogisms insofar as the number of incomplex [terms] and the quality and quantity of propositions [they contain]: "every dog runs; a heavenly constellation is a dog; therefore, a heavenly constellation runs"; "every animal is a substance; man is an animal; therefore, man is a substance"; for just as in the second syllogism the major [premise] is universal and the minor is indefinite, and just as that same predicate and not a different predicate is found in the major [premise] and in the conclusion, and the subject of the minor [premise] is found as the subject of the conclusion, and no determination [or qualification] is found in the premises that is not in the conclusion and vice versa, so is it in the first [syllogism].[54] And yet the first is a paralogism and the second is not, for this reason alone, that in the first there is an ambiguous expression which is not in the second. That said, either this ambiguity arises because some word, which is not a complete expression, is taken ambiguously, and then it is an instance of the fallacy of equivocation provided the spoken word does not vary so much in the way it is pronounced. Or the ambiguity arises from the multiple meanings of a certain word which can be pronounced in various ways and [still] remain a word, or which can be a word and an expression depending on how it is pronounced, and then it is [the fallacy] of accent. Or the entire expression is ambiguous without any ambiguity in its parts; and this can happen in two ways: either because that expression is uniformly pronounced in both senses, and if so it is [an instance of the fallacy of] amphibology, or it is not uniformly pronounced and then it is [an instance of] the fallacy of composition and division.

But if such a discourse is not a syllogism on account of a single incongruity, then it is [an instance of] the fallacy of figure of speech; for example, this: "every

---

[54]so is it in the first: i.e., if "a heavenly constellation" is considered an indefinite affirmative form.

man is an animal; every Socrates is a man; therefore, every Socrates is an animal." For if, instead of the term "Socrates," the term "ass" were used, to which a sign [or syncategorematic qualifier] may suitably be added, the syllogism would be valid.

But if a paralogism arises in a third way, it may be attributed to the fallacy of figure of speech because if, instead of the term "Socrates," some consimilar term were used, which is capable of suppositing universally for the same [thing] in any proposition, there would be no defect. And thus, on account of this word's similarity to another, someone can be deceived by the fallacy of figure of speech. Hence, – because this syllogism is valid: "this is an animal; this is a man; therefore, this animal is a man" – if someone believed that this syllogism were also valid: "he says this; this is false, indicating this: what he says is false; therefore, a falsity is said by him," he would be deceived by the fallacy of figure of speech.

But if a verbal paralogism is not so much similar to a true syllogism in the number of terms and the quality and quantity of the propositions, [but] in all respects, then either there is a defect specifically in a dissimilar quality or quantity of the premises' propositions, or, because more [terms] are put to you in the conclusion than in a true syllogism, there is a defect in an excess of incomplex terms. If [there is a defect] in the first or second way, then the argument is either valid or it is not. If valid, it is the fallacy of [affirming the] consequent; if not valid, it is the fallacy of accident.

If there is an excess of terms, namely, because more incomplex [terms] are included than ought to be, due

to either something added to the premise that should
not be; or some such thing added to the conclusion,
and then, either that to which it is added is taken as
much in the premise as in the conclusion, though in
the one it is added to itself and not so in the another,
and in that case it is [an instance of] the fallacy of *secundum quid et simpliciter*; or it is added to the one in
the premise which is not included in the conclusion,
and then it is the fallacy of irrelevant conclusion.

All this can be made clear by examples of these fallacies. From which it can even be elicited how these
fallacies might be distinguished from one another, so
that although many fallacies may be present in the
same paralogism, nevertheless it is possible to discov-
er paralogisms in which no fallacies are present except the fallacy of accident and [that of affirming the]
consequent; for, wherever the premises are disposed
in figure, if there is a fallacy of [affirming the] consequent, there will also be the fallacy of accident.

To ascertain, however, whether [something] said in
an argument is a fallacy or not, it is very useful and
necessary, among other evidence, that the respondent
reply to an argument only when the opponent argues
from certain propositions using certain words that are
not varied nor transposed nor altered in any way, and
that the respondent assiduously consider whether any
of them are ambiguous because of some fallacy of
figure of speech. From there, he should consider
whether such an argument is governed by a certain
and evident rule. And then, initially, he should respond, carefully examining each case, [to determine]
whether there be a consequent, or an opposing pre-

concession, or a previously negated antecedent, so that he might always reply appropriately.

And these remarks on the topic of fallacies should suffice for now.

AND THIS CONCLUDES THE TREATISE OF LOGIC IN THREE PARTS, WITH EACH PART SEPARATED INTO BOOKS[, WITH EACH BOOK SEPARATED INTO CHAPTERS].

Other Books by the Publisher

Fanchette's Pretty Little Foot by Restif de la Bretonne

Je M'Accuse... by Léon Bloy

My Hospitals & My Prisons by Paul Verlaine

Salvation Through the Jews by Léon Bloy

Words of a Demolitions Contractor by Léon Bloy

Cellulely by Paul Verlaine

Ecclesiastical Laurels by Jacques Rochette de la Morlière

Flowers of Bitumen by Émile Goudeau

Songs for Her & Odes in Her Honor by Paul Verlaine

On Huysmans' Tomb by Léon Bloy

Ten Years a Bohemian by Émile Goudeau

The Soul of Napoleon by Léon Bloy

Blood of the Poor by Léon Bloy

Joan of Arc and Germany by Léon Bloy

A Platonic Love by Paul Alexis

The Revealer of the Globe: Christopher Columbus & His Future Beatification (Part One) by Léon Bloy

An Immodest Proposal by Dr. Helmut Schleppend

The Pornographer by Restif de la Bretonne

Style (Theory and History) by Ernest Hello